God
of Our
Silent Tears

God of Our Silent Tears

Where does suffering come from?

What kind of God would permit innocent suffering?

What good is God when we suffer?

Dan Edwards
Foreword by John Westerhoff

CATHEDRAL CENTER PRESS
LOS ANGELES

Copyright © 2013 by Dan Edwards

All rights reserved. No part of this book may be reproduced, stored in a retrieval system, or transmitted in any form by any means, electronic, mechanical, including photocopying, recording or otherwise, without the written permission of the publisher.

ISBN: 978-0-9827584-2-7

Cathedral Center Press
An imprint of the Episcopal Diocese of Los Angeles
840 Echo Park Avenue
Los Angeles, CA 90026
www.ladiocese.org

Cover photo: Inspiring sky / © Copyright Aaron Mayes. Used with permission.
Title page photo: *Angel of Grief*, a 1894 sculpture by William Wetmore Story which serves as the gravestone of the artist and his wife, Emelyn, at the Protestant Cemetery, Rome. / Einar Einarsson Kvaran aka Carptrash 17:52, 7 August 2006 (UTC), Wikimedia Commons.
Book design & production: Molly Ruttan-Moffat

To Linda,
who has held the serene center in the midst of my anxieties,
walked with me on my paths of despair,
and inspired me to get back up, time after time after time.

Table of Contents

Acknowledgements ix

Foreword by John Westerhoff. xi

Chapter One "The Numb Blow Fallen in the Stumbling
Night": Why Do We Suffer?. 1
   Reflection Questions 12
   Notes 12

Chapter Two The Natural Order Is Deadly 14
   Reflection Questions 22
   Notes 23

Chapter Three People Behaving Badly. 24
   Reflection Questions 33
   Notes 33

Chapter Four "Perverse Motives" Attributed to God
for All Manner of Suffering. 37
   Reflection Questions 58
   Notes 59

Chapter Five God May Not Be Who You Think God Is 64
   Reflection Questions 79
   Notes 79

Chapter Six Then What Do We Say About God?. 85
   Reflection Questions 99
   Notes 100

Chapter Seven Dusting Off an Ancient Riddle 104
   Reflection Questions 120
   Notes 121

TABLE OF CONTENTS

Chapter Eight The Cosmic Vortex That Swallows
Sorrow: How the Family Trinity Responds to Suffering 128
    Reflection Questions 139
    Notes 140

Chapter Nine The Serene Father: The Job-Description
Trinity and Suffering, Part 1 144
    Reflection Questions 153
    Notes 154

Chapter Ten The Compassionate Son: The Job-Description
Trinity and Suffering, Part 2 158
    Reflection Questions 168
    Notes 168

Chapter Eleven The Revitalizing Spirit: The Job-Description
Trinity and Suffering, Part 3 172
    Reflection Questions 182
    Notes 182

Chapter Twelve Mirroring God: How We Respond to Suffering 186
    Reflection Questions 198
    Notes 199

About the Author 200

Acknowledgements

I express my thanks to the Rt. Rev. Jon Bruno, Bishop of Los Angeles, who would be my personal hero even if he had not been instrumental in the publication of this book. I am also grateful for the support of Bob Williams, Molly Ruttan-Moffat, and the Cathedral Center Press for their work in getting these thoughts into book form.

Whatever is worthy in the content of *God of Our Silent Tears* owes much to the substantive theological guidance from Professor Robert Audi of Notre Dame; Professor David Kelsey of Yale Divinity School; the Rev. Doctor John Westerhoff retired from Duke Divinity School; and the Rt. Rev. Dr. J. Neil Alexander, Dean of the University of the South School of Theology.

I am also grateful to numerous friends who have encouraged me to persist in writing this book when I was much inclined to give up; to those friends who have offered editorial advice, especially Claire Novak whose professional editorial skills brought coherence to the previously unwieldy fourth chapter; to the Scripture & Tradition Class at St. Francis Church who patiently endured an earlier version of this text for a class; and to the Diocese of Nevada Pastoral Care Class who offered helpful critique of a more recent version.

I am most profoundly grateful to the people who have shared their experiences of suffering with me over the years. Their quest for meaning is the raw material of this text as well as the reason I have written it. Above all, I thank my wife, Linda, and my children, Emilie and Katie, for standing by me and upholding me through the writing of this book and more importantly through the ordeals that gave rise to it.

Foreword

BY JOHN WESTERHOFF

Formerly Professor of Theology and Christian Nurture
Duke University Divinity School

In this book, *God of Our Silent Tears*, the Rt. Rev. Dan Edwards continues an honorable tradition in the Christian Church. As a bishop in the Episcopal Church he has written a substantial work on the Church's teachings and thereby contributed to the historic role of the bishop as guardian of the faith. This seminal work is an invitation to examine our own experiences and feelings, questions and reflections, doubts and convictions in our human quest for answers to our deep need, as believers in Jesus Christ and members of His church, to understand God and suffering.

God of Our Silent Tears is also an invitation to engage in conversations with the church's theologians who have struggled through out history with the question of how suffering forces us to rethink our understanding of the Christian faith and what it has to say about the nature and character of God, and about the purposes and destiny of human beings. As such it is not a book for the fainthearted or those who want simple answers to complex questions. Neither is it a book for those in search of certainty or those who reject the notion that doubt is a necessary dimension of faith. Rather, it is addressed to all those who believe that theological reflection which engages both the imagination and reason is possible and valuable for all the baptized. This and other books like it are needed badly in our day. One of the church's greatest failings is in the education of its laity and the continuing education of its clergy.

More than 50 years ago I was ordained as a parish priest who understood his calling as being a pastor and teacher, a symbol bearer of the church's priesthood of all believers. While always serving in a congregation I have spent a major portion of my time in the academy as theologian, lecturer, and author in the United States and throughout the world. My calling was simply to prepare future clergy for their responsibilities as teacher and prepare the laity for their calling to live into their baptismal vows and covenant. Following retirement as professor of theology and Christian nurture at Duke Divinity School, I have been a part-time parish priest, a resident theologian, and educator. Immediately after retirement I became founding director of the ecumenical St. Luke's Institute for Pastoral Studies in Atlanta, Georgia, serving both the laity and clergy. It was in this role that my life and Dan's crossed. Dan had grown up in Texas and practiced law before becoming an Episcopal priest. I first met him when he was rector of St. Francis' Episcopal Church in Macon, Georgia. The discipline of spiritual direction was being reborn, and I wanted to offer a program for the training of lay persons and clergy in spiritual direction. Impressed by his talent and knowledge in the field I invited Dan to be an instructor in one of the courses. Dan proved to be an exemplary scholar-teacher who could make profound subjects understandable. Through the years we have become colleagues and friends. He is now the bishop of Nevada and this is his first major book. I was honored and pleased to be invited to write this introduction.

Doing so was a pleasant task. I read *God of Our Silent Tears* three times, and each time I was more impressed. I am a collector and reader as well as a writer of books. Dan's *God of Our Silent Tears* has been added to my library because it makes a valuable addition to my many books on theology. Further, it is a book I can recommend to all those on a spiritual journey to rethink their image of God, as well as those who desire an aid for their pilgrimage to grow in an every deepening and loving relation to God, especially as this God is revealed as Trinity: Father, Son, and Holy Spirit.

During my life time as a priest/professor I have come to the conclusion that the greatest deterrent to the human quest for wholeness, health, and well being has been unhealthy images of God. Through the years I have been with many searching people who confessed they were having difficulty believing in God. I learned to ask them all the same question, namely, tell me about the God you do not believe in. In every case I was able to say, "I do not believe in that God either. Would you like to hear about my God?"

Indeed, I have become aware of a growing numbers of Christians who had been raised and nurtured in biblically literalistic, socially conservative, theologically fundamentalist communities and were now in search of new understandings for their deep and abiding faith in the Gospel.

Often in my experience the new Christianity they are searching for is the Christianity I first discovered at Harvard Divinity School in the early '50s. It is a faith that is new to them and expresses itself in ways that are uniquely theirs and relevant to our day and to their lives in the church.

I have come to believe that the crisis that faces the church today is a crisis of faith. While this crisis often surfaces as differing convictions concerning human sexuality, I suggest that the church is really being torn apart by radically different images of God. By focusing on suffering, I believe that Dan has written a significant book that can help all of us reflect on these differences concerning the nature and character of God and therefore how we are to live our lives faithful to God's will.

I have no need to provide the reader with an outline of the book. Dan does that in his first chapter. But I will mention his extremely helpful annotated bibliography. If the reader is intrigued by any of his insights he provides practical help on where to go next. Further his questions at the end of each chapter can aid both personal reflection and group conversation, making this book a valuable resource for adult education.

God of Our Silent Tears is itself an introduction to theology — reflections and conversations about God — for both lay persons and clergy, ordinary folk and academics. It is an invitation to participate in a personal quest to make sense of our Christian faith understood as numerous possible perceptions about God and evil, about our human desire to have a God who is in charge and why it is so difficult to believe in such a God. This is, therefore, a book for everyone who has ever wondered about human suffering, who God is and how God is with us when we suffer. It is a personal testimony by a bishop of the church that introduces us to his spiritual pilgrimage in search of a connection between the church's abstract doctrine of the Trinity and our striving to believe in a good God in a cruel world.

While I did not find anything theologically new in this book, I was enabled to remember old theological arguments better and more clearly. I was also stimulated to ask old questions in new ways and discover for myself some new answers to old questions. I found myself once again engulfed by conversations and arguments of great significance. And so I remain both inspired and grateful for Dan's invitation to share in his theological quest.

While centered in history *God of Our Silent Tears* is an original and contemporary exploration into one of the most haunting issues of our day. I trust that you will find it as stimulating as I have.

The 14th Sunday after Pentecost in Ordinary Time 2012

CHAPTER ONE

'The numb blow fallen in the stumbling night': Why do we suffer?

With these hands I lifted him from his cradle, tiny then, soft and warm, and squirming with life. Now at the end with these same hands I touched him in his coffin.
— Nicolas Wolterstorff, *Lament for a Son*

If I knew! If I knew why!
What I can't bear is . . . the blindness . . .
Meaninglessness . . . the numb blow
Fallen in the stumbling night.
— Archibald MacLeish, *J. B.*

When I walked into her hospital room, the young woman was lying there in her hospital gown, her forehead damp from the physical ordeal of labor and delivery, her cheeks damp from the tears. She reached her hands toward me and called out a single desperate question: "Why?" The stark simplicity of her question made it huge, absolutely impossible. It haunts me now, a decade later. I said, "I don't know."

Months earlier the couple announced they were expecting their first child. As their priest, I was looking forward to the baptism. But at the end of a full-term normal pregnancy, the baby was born dead. And her mother wanted to know why.

The pregnancy had gone smoothly. The baby girl had seemed healthy. There was no sign of any pathology at the birth. The baby was simply dead. In the absence of any other explanation for a stillbirth, doctors say, "It was a cord accident." Maybe it was. But that answer is just something for doctors to say. When there is no other explanation for a stillbirth, "cord accident" is the default diagnosis, not a verifiable fact. It doesn't really answer anything. If the doctors cannot give a reliable medical explanation, how is a pastor to decipher the mystery of death? Still, I would have given a fortune for something — anything — to say. I had no theological equivalent of "a cord accident." So I said, "I don't know."

WANTING OUR FAITH TO MAKE SENSE

When life disappoints us deeply in ways that make so little sense, we ask "why?" For those who believe in God, senseless sorrow shakes our faith. We lose not only a child, a lover, a hope, but also our sense that life is good and meaningful. We lose our faith. We want faith to make sense. We need our beliefs to be reasonable so we can trust them. Disasters don't fit with our trust in God's benevolent care. They make belief in an all-powerful loving God appear absurd.

Philosophers and theologians call the disconnect between faith in God and all the bad things that happen "the problem of evil." Right off, we have trouble with the vocabulary because philosophers and theologians use the word "evil" with a special meaning. Most people today use "evil" to mean seriously immoral behavior. In ordinary speech, we would not use the word "evil" to describe a medical condition or a natural disaster. But traditionally, "evil" has meant anything that is not as it ought to be. It could mean any kind of "bad" — bad weather, bad health, bad luck. "Evil" is very much like "malignant." In the law "malignant" means something akin to malice; but in medicine a cancerous tumor is called "malignant." Similarly, "evil" can be used both in moral and other ways. The term an "evil day" in times past meant a day with bad weather or a day on which an army was defeated.

That is how the philosophers and theologians use the word. So when we talk about "evil," we mean sickness, natural disasters, and misfortune as well as people doing cruel things to each other. Rabbi Kushner used the phrase "bad things." This book will use a variety of words to describe a variety of "bad things," but it will also use "evil," the way philosophers and theologians have been using it since the 1700s, as an umbrella concept to include all of them.

"The problem of evil" challenges faith. The challenge goes like this: "If God is omnipotent and God is good, then why is there evil in the world?"[1] Logically, it would seem that one of the following must be true: (1.) God is not all-powerful; (2.) God is not all good; (3.) there is not really any evil in the world.[2] You see "the problem of evil" is a serious threat to the faith of those who believe in a loving God. The poet Czeslaw Milosz puts it better:

All my life I tried to answer the question,
where does evil come from?
Impossible that people should suffer so much, if God is in Heaven
And nearby.[3]

The problem of evil has been called "the rock of atheism." Atheistic philosophers from David Hume in the 18th century to John Mackie in our day have argued that this "problem of evil" makes belief in God irrational.[4] Theologian Gordon Kaufman, summed it up: "In the face of death camps, hydrogen bombs, and napalm, of unbearably painful and destructive diseases, of impersonal calamities and unmerited suffering, how can one say that the Ruler of the world is good, loving, or merciful . . .? The particularly overwhelming evils of the 20th century have brought home this dimension of the problem of God with renewed force."[5] Bart Ehrman's book *God's Problem* is his account of how the horrible things that happen to people make it impossible for him to believe in God.

OUR FIRST INNER CONFLICT:
DO WE WANT TO BELIEVE GOD IS IN CHARGE?

The "problem of evil" runs deeper in our hearts than a logical conundrum in our heads. It is a matter of our conflicted longing. Do we want to believe God is in charge of what is happening or not? The "problem of evil," at the feeling level, lies in our conflicted desires. On the one hand, we want God to intervene — to part the Red Sea when it blocks our way, to heal our diseases, cast out our demons, and raise our dead. We need help finding our car keys, paying our bills, and keeping our tempers. We want a higher power to liberate us from alcohol. We want to turn it over, to let go and let God. All of that requires God to be both powerful and actively involved in our lives, even arranging occasional miracles to save our necks.

On the other hand, if God is powerful enough and involved enough to help us, then aren't our problems his fault to begin with? Where was God when things went wrong? If God can help us, why hasn't he already done it? What kind of a God would insist that we crawl and beg before he helps, and sometimes he won't help even then. Better to think God is powerless or uninvolved. Such a God would be innocent and perhaps likeable, but not particularly important or even relevant to our lives.

Then to confuse things further, miracle, wonder, and serendipity come along. Grace happens just often enough that we can't dismiss the notion that God may be lending us a hand on occasion. Why then does God act only on occasion? Believing God could deliver us from suffering actually implicates God in our suffering. A man trapped in the World Trade Center on September 11 prayed to be saved. He was saved, but his response wasn't gratitude. This is his story:

> "Lord help me please," he prayed, the primal prayer. "Then," he said, "I feel like this strange force came over me, that I never felt before... and I busted a little hole [and crawled out]... My Lord upheld this building. Then we were in perfect safety, and the building collapsed. And here I am. God delivered. And I'm angry. Angry because all these good people who were there, all these good people were left in this building. So I'm angry."[6]

If God can save but doesn't, we have to blame him. But blaming God for suffering is problematic. If God is our ideal, our highest concept, what we strive to resemble, then blaming God for suffering actually corrupts our souls. Emulating the person we blame is a mind-twister, so we are inclined to say God cannot do anything about real world problems.

Despairing of God's ability to do anything about our suffering is practical atheism. God may exist but he does not matter. I know two people who each lost a child to death. One of them dealt with his loss by trusting that God caused his daughter's early death for a greater good. The other bereaved parent exonerated God of her child's death, insisting God does not run the world. Their opposite answers each helped them cope for awhile, but neither answer was truly adequate. The first answer made God a killer. The second made God a helpless bystander. Which one deserves our worship?

We can escape this dilemma by simply rejecting God. Indeed, if we want to reject God, the persistence of misfortune can give us reason to do so. We can say there is no God or that God is not good. Those responses, however, are not particularly helpful when it comes to

THE NUMB BLOW FALLEN IN THE STUMBLING NIGHT: WHY DO WE SUFFER?

finding ways to survive, to find the meaning in our experiences, or to overcome the obstacles that hold us back in life.

Perhaps the "overwhelming evils of the 20th century" may lead us to re-think who God is instead of giving up on faith and succumbing to despair. This book will present such an alternative. Instead of using life's sorrow as an occasion to deny God, we will *reconsider who God is*. We will use this occasion to find a truer, more praiseworthy God, a God who will empower us to overcome hardship and affliction.

OUR SECOND INNER CONFLICT: DO WE REALLY WANT AN ANSWER TO THE QUESTION 'WHY'?

There is another matter of the heart that makes it exceedingly difficult to come to terms with tragedy. On the one hand, we desperately need to makes sense of what has happened; on the other hand, we refuse to make sense of it because that implies accepting things

Photo: Sorrow. / © Copyright Timothy S. March 1987. Used with permission.

we know are unacceptable. We are torn. Let's look at both sides of this inner conflict.

Finding meaning in tragedy is vital if we are to keep breathing and putting one foot in front of the other. Victor Frankl learned an important lesson as a death camp prisoner in World War II: the people most likely to survive were those who managed to find some meaning in their struggle. So Frankl developed new kind of psychotherapy that consisted of helping people find the positive value in their pain.[7] People survive by making some kind of sense of even the most senseless things that happen to us. Christians look to God for an explanation. We look to God to redeem our loss with a plan that leads to a greater good. Countless Christians over the centuries have consoled themselves at gravesides with such phrases as "It's God's will" or "The Lord giveth and the Lord taketh away."

But there is another side of this dilemma to consider. Can we love a Lord who "giveth and taketh away" in arbitrary and sometimes cruel ways? Do such platitudes urge us to accept things we should not accept, things our hearts rebel against. Dostoevsky's character Ivan Karamazov refused to accept religious justifications for the unspeakable suffering he saw. In an argument with his pious brother, Aloysha, Ivan rejected faith for this precise reason.

For the sake of argument, he conceded that maybe, in some mysterious way, God will someday make everything wonderful. He even conceded, for the sake of argument, that the sufferings people endure now are in some unknown way a necessary part of the plan that will lead to cosmic bliss for all. Even so, he found God immoral for using suffering to accomplish his ends. Ivan refused to be complicit in God's immorality by accepting grace through faith. He recounted cases of children brutally tortured and murdered. Even if all will be set right and healed someday, and even if these atrocities were somehow necessary to an eternal harmony, Ivan insisted, that makes God no less monstrous.

"I challenge you, let's assume you were called upon to build the edifice of human destiny so that men would finally be happy and find tranquility. If you knew that, in order to attain this, you would have to torture just one single creature, let's say the little girl who beat her breast so desperately in the outhouse, and that on her unavenged tears you could build that edifice, would you do it? Tell me and do not lie!"

"No, I would not," Aloysha said softly.

> "And do you find acceptable the idea that those for whom you are building that edifice should gratefully receive a happiness that rests on the blood of a tortured child and, having received it, should continue to enjoy it eternally?"

Dostoevsky and Frankl represent the two sides of a basic dilemma. Frankl rightly says that we must find meaning in our affliction if we are to survive it. Dostoevsky protests that the horrors people too often face cannot be justified with any overarching meaning.

A clear example of this conflict is the difference among Jews over what to call the genocide their forebears suffered at the hands of Hitler. Some use the word *holocaust*, the word for a sacrifice or offering, a word that suggests there is some spiritual meaning to be found even in the depths of this atrocity. Others use the word *shoah*, which means disaster or catastrophe. The word *shoah* insists there is nothing good to be found in such evil. We will not stand for such horrors to be defended or justified by any transcendent meaning.

WHAT THIS BOOK WILL AND WILL NOT DO

So what will this book offer for the person struggling to make sense of the "tears in the nature of things" as Samuel Taylor Coleridge called it? Let's put that question on the table now.

I have written this book because the current conversation over the problem of evil is lopsided. The atheist voices, such as Bart Ehrman in *God's Problem*, state their case with a simple logic supported by powerful examples of how horrible things can be while God does nothing, if there is a God at all. The Christian voice in reply often turns to psychology, reflects back feelings, offers a caring presence. Providing pastoral care is exactly what Christians should do. But when people are up against the existential question of whether life can be meaningful, whether life is worthwhile, they need more than a caring presence — they need some answers. When they are up against the religious questions, "Does God exist?" "Does God matter?" "Is God even good?" they need answers.

This book responds to the questions they rightly ask. It is for thinking about suffering. It is theological, not psychological or devotional. Theology engages our minds to make sense of faith in a world that sometimes seems senseless. In these pages we will talk back to Ehrman, Hitchens, Dawkins, and their predecessors Hume

and Mackey. We will show how faith is possible in the face of tragedy. But this is not the same thing as offering a tidy explanation of things. Our answer will be humbler and more nuanced than that. It has to be if we are going to tell the truth.
Will we explain and justify the suffering in the world? There are explanations of evil and suffering in the Christian tradition. We will consider those answers because most of them contain some truth. They are, however, at best partial explanations. We can offer explanations that help a little, but ultimately do not solve the problem. As philosopher Marilyn McCord Adams notes:

> ... (T)he pressure to provide rationales (for evil) ... drives us to advance credible partial reasons ... as total explanations, thereby exacerbating the problem of evil by attributing perverse motives to God.[8]

We don't want to "attribute perverse motives to God" because we cannot and should not worship and obey someone with perverse motives.

There are two reasons we will not offer a solid answer to the question of why "bad things" happen. First, we don't have one to offer. We have some insights — but not a comprehensive answer. Let me be clear that taking God out of the equation doesn't solve anything either. If we deny God's existence, that changes the logical structure of the problem, but it does not give us an explanation of suffering. Evil is even more mysterious without God.

Second, we don't want to offer such an answer because to fully and satisfactorily explain evil would be to justify it. We don't want to do that. We want to preserve the human voice of rebellion that says "No. This will not do." We honor the voice that remembers the holocaust. We do not want to justify the holocaust. We want to join the voices of those who say, "Never again!"

Will we offer a reasonable grounds for faith in the face of horror and tragedy? Yes. We will offer a way of thinking about God that is credible and helpful. But it will not be God as so many philosophers have defined "God" in "the problem of evil" literature. It will not be the understanding of God that many believers hold today. We will reach back to an older, truer, and better way of understanding God. We will discover images of God that console, sustain and inspire. It will not be the patriarchal God, the God of omnipotent domination. That is the God who makes "the problem of evil" intractable. If we are to grapple with our affliction creatively, it will be necessary for us to break out of the mental box of the logical problem of evil. It is built on misconceptions about God—misconceptions we must cast aside if we are to examine how the Triune God of the Christian tradition responds to us in our hour of need. In this book, we will rediscover the Triune God espoused by Christians in the first centuries of their faith, a mystical cosmic dance of a God, who heals, restores, and redeems.

IS THIS BOOK FOR YOU?

If you are looking for a simple explanation of suffering, a fast-acting comfort, or a quick bandage to a life-wound, no. The answers this book will explore are not simple and offer no palliative. If you are looking for a pastoral care manual, a list of comforting aphorisms to say in a crisis situation, this is not your book. We will be struggling with partial answers and re-thinking basic assumptions. This is a book to read before you are in crisis or after the crisis is passed and you are in the longer, slower process of finding meaning in it.

But if your own suffering or the suffering you see in the world shakes your faith, or if you want to discover what your faith can offer a world in pain, then, yes, this book is for you. If you have friends whose faith has been destroyed by "the problem of evil," and you want to engage them in constructive conversation, then yes, this book is for you. Perhaps you have read Bart Ehrman's book *God's Problem* and found your faith unsettled by his arguments against faith. This book is for you.

If you want to know more about a Christian view of who God is and how God is connected to this life of mixed joy and sorrow, then, yes, this book is for you. You may discover here a Christianity you did not know existed. More surprising still, you will hear that what you may have assumed is the Christian party line is utterly contrary to the ancient Christian tradition and to the views of leading Christian theologians today. This book is about God considered in light of a central question in life: why do we suffer? That question leads inexorably to God. It makes us think seriously about who God is. The fact of suffering makes many beliefs about God impossible, including some beliefs that are widely held. Suffering may also open the way for us to believe in God in better ways, to see God as better than we knew God to be, more worthy of our worship. Theologian Jurgen Moltmann expresses the connection between God and suffering this way:

> God and suffering belong together.... The question about God and the question about suffering are a joint, a common question. And they only find a common answer. Either that, or neither of them finds a satisfactory answer at all.[9]

And philosopher Michael Peterson echoes, "(W)hat a religious system says about evil reveals a great deal about what it takes ultimate reality and humanity's relationship to it to be."[10]

If, for any reason, you want to explore the question of why God allows things to fall into such misery and disarray, then this book is for you. My hope for you is that, when you have finished *God of Our Silent Tears*, you will have a deeper sense of who God is and how God is with us in our hardest hours. I hope that this sense of God will deepen your assurance, will give you resilience, and inspire you to live your own life more courageously while responding to the suffering of others compassionately. I hope that this deepened sense of God will strengthen you to act for the alleviation of misery and for the rectification of injustice. My hope for you, whoever you are, is that this book will contribute to your growth in wisdom and love for God and for all creation.

This is a book of Christian theology, but you do not have to be a Christian to find value in it. Christian language can often be translated into the language and imagery of other traditions. If you are from another faith tradition, do not think that I am rejecting your tradition. I am just speaking my own language. The conversation here is not essentially an interfaith dialogue. My goal is to clarify Christianity. That will involve repudiating some erroneous and frankly pathological versions of Christianity. If you are from another faith tradition, this book is not written to challenge your way. But if you are a Christian, you are at risk in this book. You will likely hear some of your assumptions directly challenged.

If you are committed to believing that Christian tradition is oppressive and that truth and mercy are the exclusive province of the outsiders, you will be discomfited by my reliance on ancient teachers and creeds. I am reasserting orthodox teaching, though I hope it is, to use Brian McLaren's apt phrase, "a generous orthodoxy." If you think orthodox faith is the rigid judgmental brand of Christianity which is so prominent in the media, you will not find that here. The doctrines here are an orthodoxy reclaimed by feminist and liberation theologians.

AN OVERVIEW OF THE BOOK

Chapters 2-4 will present the traditional theories about why God causes or allows evil to happen, explaining and evaluating the theories as we go. There is a germ of truth in most of them, but ultimately they are not adequate. Christianity does not explain, defend, or justify the existence of evil. Instead, Christianity portrays a God who offers healing and hope in our times of despair.

The book then turns to rethinking who God is and what God is like. The problem of evil is based on a certain way of imagining God, a way which is not the ancient understanding, does not make sense, and is not helpful to suffering people.

Finally, I will tell you about an older, wiser, truer way of understanding God. You may be surprised that I want to reclaim the traditional doctrine of the Holy Trinity, but I have a compelling reason: this understanding of God offers a foundation for hope. I want to share with you what I have learned in my own journey searching for a good God in a cruel world. I have found such a God. My belief in this God is more than an opinion. It is a conviction, a matter of trust.[11] I want to share my belief because it offers comfort and hope. The God I believe in is the God who sustained African Americans through their ordeals of slavery and segregation, who consoled them but also gave them hope for a better life, who empowered them to struggle against injustice. The God I believe in is the God described by the great Black poet James Weldon Johnson:

God of our weary years,
God of our silent tears,
Thou who hast brought us thus far on the way;
Thou who hast by thy might,
Led us into the light,
Keep us forever on the path, we pray.[12]

This God inspires and empowers people to respond to the suffering of others with compassion. I want to share this belief because

I find it beautiful. It's the ground on which I stand. I stake my life on it, trusting not only that it is true but also that it is the way through suffering, injustice, and violence.

REFLECTION QUESTIONS

1. How would you answer Ivan's question to Aloysha? Is it moral to accept admission to a paradise bought with blood of a tortured child? Is it moral to accept admission to a paradise bought with the blood of Jesus?

2. Do you believe evil, suffering and misfortune happen in the world? Might it be an illusion?

3. If you have to choose between believing that God is good and believing that God is omnipotent, which one would you choose?

NOTES

[1] Philosophers of religion may present this problem in terms of God's omniscience as much as God's omnipotence. From that perspective, the question is, "If God knew this would happen, why did he create such a world?" This is a profound question. It goes to the question of ultimate meaning that the philosopher must ask. But we will focus on omnipotence since it is the characteristic of God that affects our immediate relationship with God and our immediate relationship with suffering. We want to know whether God can do anything for us, and if so, why doesn't he do it?

[2] This is a simplified version of the problem. A full statement includes God's existence and omniscience. The atheist argues that these propositions are logically inconsistent. There are also three version of the final element: (a.) evil exists; (b.) large amounts, extreme kinds, and perplexing distributions of evil exist; (c.) gratuitous or pointless evil exists. Michael L.

Peterson, *God And Evil* (Boulder: Westview Press, 1998) pp. 23-24. Marilyn McCord Adams, *Horrendous Evils And The Goodness Of God* (Ithaca: Cornell University Press, 1999), p. 9.

3   Czeslaw Milosz, "High Terraces," in *Second Space*, trans. Czeslaw Milosz and Robert Haas (New York: Harper Collins, 2004), p. 22.

4   Michael L. Peterson, pp. 17-18. Anthony Flew has more recently changed his mind on these issues and converted to theism.

5   Gordon Kaufman, *God The Problem* (Cambridge: Harvard University Press, 1972), p. 13.

6   Andrew Silver, "Prayer In A Minor Key," unpublished manuscript. January 2006.

7   Victor Frankl, *Man's Search For Meaning* (New York, Beacon Press, 1959).

8   Adams, pp. 155-156.

9   Jurgen Moltmann, *The Trinity and the Kingdom*, trans. Margaret Kohl (Minneapolis: Fortress Press, 1993), p. 49.

10   Michael L. Peterson, *God And Evil* (Boulder: Westview Press, 1998), p. 7.

11   "Belief in God means trusting God, accepting Him, committing one's life to Him." Alvin C. Plantinga, *God, Freedom, and Evil* (Wm. B. Eerdmans Publishing Co., 1974), p. 2.

12   James Weldon Johnson, "Lift Every Voice And Sing," *Lift Every Voice And Sing*, ed. Horace Clarence Boyer (New York: Church Publishing Inc, 1993), p. 1.

CHAPTER TWO

The natural order is deadly

*They were confused,
the chaos too much for them
destruction as far
as 3 miles in
where are the people
hundreds of shoppers
swept from an outdoor
market. Roads
remain impassible*

*One child watches
the cremation of his
sister. And in
the pale boy's arms,
the sign: MISS PARENTS
AND TWO SISTERS*

— Lyn Lifshin, "They Were Confused, The Chaos Too Much for Them," from *Tsunami as History*

The 2004 tsunami that devastated South Asia is the largest modern natural disaster. In the midst of that catastrophe, there were stories of unlikely, seemingly miraculous survivals, like a toddler who floated on a mattress for five hours before she was rescued. But more than 100,000 people were not rescued. The waters tore a six month old Australian baby, Melina Heppell, from her father's arms. Tamara Mendis, the wife of a Chicago Lutheran pastor, was visiting her family in Sri Lanka when the waters overwhelmed her train and took her life. To say Melina and Tamara were in the wrong place at the wrong time doesn't begin to explain why any place should undergo such a time.

"The problem of evil" arises out of certain assumptions that if there is a God, then God is a certain way. God is the all-powerful designer, manufacturer and ruler of the world. God is loving, good and kind. Up against that, we experience a world in which horrible things happen. Everything must be the way God wants it. Then why are things so bad? All of the attempted answers to that question have a name — "theodicy."[1] It means, in the words of John Milton, "to justify the ways of God to man." We will begin by examining the main theodicies of Christian tradition, the main ways Christian theologians have tried to make sense of this conundrum.

WHAT IS NATURAL EVIL?

Theologians divide the "bad things" into two categories and then give them special names: *natural evil* and *human evil*. "Natural evil" refers to destructive events that happen without respect to human conduct or decisions — like hurricanes, earthquakes, tsunamis, cancer, and birth defects. In the face of "natural evil," they ask such questions as, "Why do people have to endure paralysis from strokes and multiple sclerosis, dementia, crippling arthritis? Why is there famine?" Philosophers and theologians distinguish these "bad things" from "human evil" which refers to destructive actions by human beings — like terrorism, the holocaust, slavery, crime, discrimination, and neglect of the poor. The pain caused by a tumor impinging on a nerve and the pain inflicted by a sadistic torturer are both pain. Our bodies process them in similar ways. But to our hearts and our minds, these two pains are altogether different and demand different responses.

We may quibble with the semantics. The word "evil" may or may not be appropriate for things that happen in nature. Nature is not a moral agent. The distinction between natural evil and human evil gets blurred in some cases. But I will use the two terms because they are generally accepted in theological circles and because some explanations may fit one kind of problem but not the other. We can't explain natural suffering like a tsunami the same way we explain a mass murder. Nature does not function with a will the way people do. So theology treats natural suffering differently.

I take up natural evil first because it is the kind of evil most often and most readily attributed to God. When people hurt each other, we can blame the people. But when nature hurts us, we have no one to blame but God.

BEING MORTAL AND VULNERABLE

After the funeral, the mourners gather
under the rustling churchyard maples
and talk softly, like clusters of leaves . . .
They came this afternoon to say goodbye,
but now they keep saying hello and hello,
peering into each other's faces,
slow to let go of each other's hands.
— Ted Kooser, "Mourners," from *Delights and Shadows*

The basic problem is that we are not God. As creatures, we are mortal, so we die. Sad as that may be, it is just how it is. But why can't God make us immortal? One reason is that life is meaningful only if it is made up of real choices. Without death, we do not really have to make choices. Having only one limited life to live means our choices count. Only if choices count, only if they really are choices from among a limited number of opportunities, do we have real freedom. Mortality is the tragic but essential context for authentic human life.

Not only does mortality make life choices meaningful, it makes life precious. In Marilynne Robinson's novel *Gilead*, when old pastor Ames is approaching death, he says,

I feel sometimes as if I were a child who opens its eyes on the world once and sees amazing things it will never know any names for and then has to close its eyes again. I know all this is all a mere apparition compared to what awaits us, but it is only lovelier for that. There is a human beauty to it. And I can't believe that when we have been changed and put on incorruptibility that we will forget our fantastic condition of mortality and impermanence, the great bright dream of procreating and perishing that meant the whole world to us. In eternity, this world will be Troy . . . and all that has passed here will be the epic of the universe, the song they sing in the streets.[2]

Our mortal, vulnerable condition makes life precious and beautiful. It makes our choices meaningful. Some forms of suffering (loneliness, limitation, temptation, and anxiety) "belong to the human condition." They are necessary to all that we value and love in life. They are inherent in being human and essential to our fulfilling our spiritual potential. Theologian Douglas John Hall calls these hardships "integrative suffering."[3]

Frailty, faults, and death make compassion possible. They are the context of personal relationships that could not exist among more angelic beings. As Czeslaw Miloz writes in his poem "In a Parish,"

Had I not been frail and half broken inside
I would not think of them,
who are like myself half broken inside.
I would not climb the cemetery hill by the church
To get rid of my self-pity.
Crazy Sophies.
Michaels who lost every battle,
Self-destructive Agathas
Lie under crosses with their dates of
birth and death,
And who is going to express them?
Their mumblings, weepings, hopes,
tears of humiliation? . . .

There is some truth in the idea that mortality gives makes life precious, poignant and meaningful. It is also true that vulnerability is essential to truly human relationship. Spiritual teachers from several traditions have prescribed practicing awareness of our impending death as a way to sharpen our appreciation of life. "Keep death at your left shoulder," some say. "*Memento mori*" — "remember death," we used to inscribe on tombstones.

But that argument only defends the fact that life is subject to some limits. It does not justify the extent of human suffering or the randomness with which people die. It does not justify life ending prematurely or slowly with frailty and senility. It does not justify pain and disability. Much of our vulnerability is quite unnecessary to make life meaningful and beautiful. The Christian tradition does not posit, in Hall's words, "a God who actually wills the massive, unbearable, or seemingly absurd suffering of the creature — *any* creature! A deity personally and directly responsible for all the agony of earth would be unrecognizable as God from the perspective of biblical faith."[4]

Photo: The immediate aftermath of the earthquake in Haiti.
© Copyright www.zoriah.net. Used with permission.

NATURAL LAW

Life depends on natural law. We need gravity, and we need it to be constant, dependable. Otherwise any step we take might propel us into outer space. The price of gravity is that if we fall off the ledge of a skyscraper, we are going to get hurt. The same natural laws that kill us are also essential to our lives. The same properties of water that make it life-sustaining make it capable of drowning us. When nature hurts or kills us, it is nature doing it — not God personally selecting us for calamity. God made nature the way it is, dangerous, because the laws that threaten us are necessary for us to be here at all.

If we give God credit for making a world where life is possible, do we also have to blame God for making a world where disease, injury, and death are inevitable? It depends on whether one could really create a world without polarities: yin without yang, day without night, life without death. The possibility of such a different universe is highly speculative.

The universe is structured as it is, a mix of order and chaos, a universe that miraculously generates and sustains living, sentient beings, but in which things tend to fall apart. Scientists call it entropy. St. Paul said in Romans Chapter 8 that the cosmos is subjected to "futility," to "bondage to decay." The tendency of things to fall apart is a law of physics, the second law of thermodynamics. It corresponds with the Second Noble Truth of Buddhism. Things fade, crumble and die. This universe generates life, but the life it generates is vulnerable and ultimately, inescapably mortal.

We may try to imagine some other universe, a realm of life without death, a universe operating according to utterly different physics in which things would not fall apart, natural law would never get in our way, and random accidents would be impossible. However, if we try to actually flesh out our fantasy universe, we find it very hard to create a coherent picture of it even in make-believe. Why then do we think God could make a dramatically different universe? Some philosophers have argued that the world we have may not be ideal but it is "the best of all possible worlds."[5] This may or may not be "the best of all possible worlds," but the idea that it could have been made significantly better is speculation, not a verifiable truth.

The natural law explanation is, nonetheless, troublesome. First, we have to remember the flesh-and-blood situations that raise the question "why" and the flesh-and-blood people who ask it. Does it help to tell them they are just cogs in the machine of a universe ruled by indifferent natural laws? This explanation does a poor job of offering meaning or value in our experience. In fact, it does quite the opposite.

The natural law explanation is also unsatisfactory as a way to understand God. It makes God a remote designer of a system left to run itself, even when it is running over us. It says God is no longer involved with our world which now runs by impersonal rules, not personal influence. God may be the Creator of such a world, but God has become largely irrelevant. It is like being God is a job he once held, but he has now retired or become a Divinity Emeritus. Can we even call such an insignificant character God? We have acquitted God of responsibility for our hardships; but at what cost? We have eliminated the God who might have offered us hope.

RANDOMNESS

Natural law is God's way of making the world orderly. But the world is not entirely orderly. There is a lot of randomness, chaos, and dumb luck. In the 17th century, science portrayed the world as quite orderly. But the science of our day, including chaos theory and Heisenberg's Indeterminacy Principle, shows us a world in which Dame Fortune is a major player. Mutations and genetic accidents may cause us to be especially gifted or horribly handicapped. We may miraculously survive an accident that ought to kill us, or we may be killed by a freak accident that shouldn't have hurt us at all. One morning in Idaho, an earthquake shook my bed. Throughout the state, there were no serious injuries — except in one town, far from the epicenter, where two elementary schoolboys were waiting for their bus. They were standing beside a wall which collapsed and killed them. Randomness.

Biologist Mary Beth Saffo observes that survival of the fittest is only one factor in evolution. Chance, which figures prominently in history, also shapes the natural order. She writes:

Happenstance, events out of the blue, circumstances beyond our control . . . ., are woven through human experience. . . If Richard III's horse had not lost his shoe, would the Tudors have come to power? How would U. S. history be different had John F. Kennedy not been assassinated? Had the Palm Beach ballots been less confusing during the 2000 presidential elections, would the United States have gone to war in Iraq? . . . Chance permeates every level of the evolutionary process. Consider the importance of mutation. Genetic variation is the raw material for evolutionary change.[6]

Like natural law, chaos and randomness are necessary to life and freedom. Without the chaos factor, we wouldn't have galaxies, solar systems, life, awareness, or civilization. A perfectly orderly distribution of matter and energy, generated from the Big Bang, would be equally spaced going straight out from Ground Zero. It might be lovely, but it would be dead. The chaos factor caused matter and energy to take an uneven course that created dust clouds, stars, planets, and ultimately the conditions for life. Irregularities and disruptions continue to play a vital role. Volcanoes, tectonic instabilities, and seismic shocks are actually essential to life on our planet. Without them we would not have the weather patterns necessary to grow crops that sustain life.

Creation consists not only of order forming out of chaos, but also of a certain amount of beneficent chaos giving life to sterile order. We need the chaos factor. But chaos is chaotic; randomness is random. It is as apt to do us harm as to do us good. Saffo points to the 2004 tsunami as "devastat[ing] societies and individual lives, in patterns that have nothing to do with justice or fairness and that even defy easy biological explanations."[7]

Here we come to an analogy between the behavior of humans and the behavior of nature. In explaining "human evil," theologians often assert "the free will defense." It goes: sin is the price we pay for human free will. Freedom makes a better humanity in the long run, even if we sometimes use our freedom to do abominable things. There is an analogy between human freedom and the random functioning of nature. We call it "the free process defense." The argument goes that we get a better world if it is in the process of making itself through "evolutionary explorations" than if God created a perfectly balanced, unchanging order.[8]

There are several problems with the free process defense. First, if (and this is a most uncertain if) God could have created a perfectly ordered cosmos that would sustain life and that would not randomly injure people, we may well wonder whether a universe with free process is actually better. Second, this explanation, like natural law, treats God as largely irrelevant to our lives. Chaos has its sphere and there doesn't appear to be much God can do about it. If chaos is more powerful than God, then does that mean Chaos is really God? Third, the value of spiritual growth through moral decision-making is clear for people, but not for tectonic plates. Nor does lethal nature, killing a village with a mudslide, make human life or the functioning of nature meaningful in the way that human freedom makes our lives meaningful. Finally, as John Polkinghorne, says, "free process" does not justify the massive scale of human suffering.

A totally risk-free world might be so bland as to fail to stimulate human spiritual growth and development. Some challenge from danger and difficulty can be seen as constituent of what it is to be human (think of dangerous pastimes such as mountain climbing). Yet the weight of suffering often seems to exceed what can be borne, crushing those on whom it falls. Some rise above the impact of evil in a way that is inspiring, but other are diminished by it almost to the point of extinction of their humanity.[9]

CONCLUSION

The basic problem is our mortality and vulnerability which are necessary to make life precious and meaningful. Natural law and natural chaos are both necessary for life, but also capable of being destructive. Yet these explanations have not proven truly satisfactory. Think back to the parents of the Australian baby drowned in the tsunami. Or think of the Lutheran pastor who lost his wife. They might readily acknowledge that a tsunami is part of the nature and that nature gives us life. But does that explanation comfort them or strengthen them to live. I doubt this is the kind of "meaning" Victor Frankl had in mind as a way to cope with tragedy. If we are going to honestly represent the nature of life and consider the causes of suffering, then we need to acknowledge what this chapter has said about nature. But we must not pretend that this has answered the anguished cry of "why?"

REFLECTION QUESTIONS

1. Do the natural law and natural chaos explanations seem true to you? Are they helpful? Why or why not?

2. What do you think of the belief that, by and large, the forces of nature are serving God's purpose even when they cause us to suffer and die? Is that belief helpful? Why or why not?

3. How would we experience life if we lived in this world forever? What would pleasure be like if there were no pain? What would joy be like if there were no sorrow? These are not rhetorical questions. Really try to imagine the situations described and answer honestly.

4. Do you believe God could have made the universe radically different from the way it is, so that there would be no suffering or death? Why or why not?

NOTES

[1] A word we owe to the 18th-century philosopher Leibniz who argued that this is the best possible world.

[2] Marilynne Robinson, *Gilead* (New York: Farrar, Straus, and Giroux, 2004), p. 57.

[3] Douglas John Hall, *God and Human Suffering* (Minneapolis: Augsburg Publishing House, 1986), p. 21.

[4] Douglas John Hall, pp. 53-62.

[5] Notably, G. W. Leibniz. Voltaire in *Candide* satirized this notion. Alvin Plantinga persuasively argues that, as a matter of logic, God could not have created the world in a radically different way, and that the mix of good and evil in the world is at least possibly as good as it can get. Plantinga, pp. 32-44; Peterson, p. 39.

[6] Mary Beth Saffo, "Accidental Elegance: How Chance Authors the Universe," *The American Scholar* Vol. 74, No. 3 (Summer, 2005), pp. 20-21, 24.

[7] Mary Beth Saffo, at pp. 20-21.

[8] "A world allowed to make itself through the evolutionary explorations of its potentiality is a better world than one produced by divine fiat. In such an evolving world there must be some malfunctions and blind alleys. The same biochemical processes which allow some cells to mutate and produce new forms of life will allow other cells to mutate and become malignant. Entities will behave in accordance with their nature, as when tectonic plates slip and cause a devastating earthquake." Polkinghorne, John. *Science and Theology: An Introduction* (Minneapolis: Fortress Press, 1998), p. 94. Robert Farrar Capon explained the great Lisbon earthquake of 1775 as God's responsibility because God made the world as it is, not "a homogeneous block of monel metal" but an unstable shell over a molten magma core. Capon relates the seeming randomness of the earth having formed in that way to the freedom of creation. Robert Farrar Capon, *The Third Peacock* (Garden City: Doubleday, 1971), pp. 35-36.

[9] Polkinghorne, p. 94.

CHAPTER 3

People behaving badly

*I was in a class
and the teacher said
I hear we hear we have
a Jew pig in this class.
I shook. He said
I'm going to show
this Jew pig
how much pain
a Jew can survive.
He took a stick
out of the desk
and hit and hit.
I don't remember the pain,
but only the kids
who'd once been my friends
laughing and laughing.*
    — Lyn Lifshin, "For Me the Holocaust Started in '33
     in a Small Village" from *Blue Tattoo*[1]

People do horrid things to each other. The point is too obvious to belabor. The question is why are we as we are? Why does God allow us to hurt each other? Why did God design people to be so vulnerable and so violent? Perhaps we may say that human beings are responsible for our own conduct, but does that let God off the hook? Doesn't our maker share some of the blame?

Sometimes, even the perpetrators of evil are mystified. In 2005, an incarcerated man, Brian Nichols, was at the Atlanta courthouse for a hearing in his case. He was to stand trial for rape. He escaped from his jailer and took her gun. Rather than take the direct route of escape, he wandered through the courthouse looking for his courtroom. He found it and shot to death the judge and the court reporter. He later said the judge had never treated him unfairly. He had no grudge against the court reporter. He just killed them. He then went on a series of car-jackings in his escape. In the course of his rampage through the city, he killed two more people. That night he forced his way into an apartment and held the young woman there hostage, doing her no harm. They watched the news together. Nichols saw himself on television and was completely perplexed. He knew he had in fact committed these crimes. He saw himself on television committing some of them. He remembered them. And yet it did not seem to him that he was the one who had done it. It was as if he had been someone else. His only explanation was that as he sat in jail awaiting trial and saw that most of the other people were of his race, he was enraged by institutional racism. Yet he killed people toward whom he harbored no personal malice. His story may represent the shadow side of racism. But it is ultimately unexplained. The only one with inside knowledge does not understand it himself. Nichols may well be incarcerated, perhaps even executed — but can the force that drove him to kill be so easily constrained or eradicated? What drives people to do things that don't make sense even to them?

One explanation is that God makes people do evil for some secret greater good. The widow of the judge Bryan Nichols killed said,

I think of (Bryan Nichols) as a modern day Judas. Judas was a person God used to carry out his wishes. God really could have put it in the mind of Nichols to go a different route, take a different door, not even go there. But he didn't. I live by a fact that this had to be for a reason.[2]

While one has to sympathize with any widow struggling to come to terms with her husband's sudden and violent death, we must resist the notion that criminals are God's "Manchurian Candidates" going about killing, raping, and torturing to "carry out God's wishes." Unless we accept the image of God as a cosmic mobster boss, we are left to look for other explanations of why God would allow people to behave so cruelly.

FREE WILL

Why, then do bad things happen to good people? One reason is that our being human leaves us free to hurt each other, and God can't stop us without taking away the freedom that makes us human.
— Harold Kushner, *When Bad Things Happen to Good People*[3]

The "free will defense" is easily the most widely held belief explaining why an omnipotent good God would allow people to misbehave. The argument goes that freedom is essential to make life meaningful and valuable. We are given freedom so our relationship with God can be personal and authentic. God wants real lovers, not "Stepford Wives". The price of freedom is the genuine possibility that freedom will be abused. Free persons will sometimes choose to do wrong.

Philosopher Alvin Plantinga has made a cogent argument that evil is the price of freedom and that a free world is better than a world that is good only because it has no choice.[4] Freedom makes the whole event of human life meaningful as opposed to a puppet show. Spiritually, the value of freedom is even greater. One of the most compelling views of our world is as an arena for "soul making." In such an arena, freedom to choose between good and evil is essential to the environment for spiritual growth.[5] As a matter of philosophical logic, the "free will defense" is widely regarded as having carried the day against the atheist argument based on the problem of human evil.[6]

While this "free will defense" does not help with natural evil, it is so persuasive in explaining human evil that we need to be careful not to swallow it whole before we have chewed on it a bit. Oddly enough this popular notion, in its current form, is fairly new. Augustine said that creation was given a primal freedom for the sake of making the whole project meaningful. However, that freedom was lost with the fall of Adam. Since then, the creation has been decidedly unfree because it is enslaved to the power of sin.

While "free will" resonates with the cultural assumptions of modern Westerners who vote for political candidates and routinely choose from among five different brands of laundry detergent, most Christians through history have not shared these assumptions. Trumpeting even the existence of individual free will was called "the Arminian heresy" well into the 18th century. Christians traditionally might have believed with Augustine in "free Fall," that creation and humanity were free in the beginning, but that did not mean humanity was still free to choose between good and evil. Rather humanity was enslaved to evil, and awaiting liberation.

St. Paul did not regard sin as a wrong moral choice. He regarded it as a power to which people are in bondage. He said of himself that he did not do the good he wanted to do, but compulsively did the evil he did not want to do.[7] Just so, in our time, contemporary theologians have disputed the free will defense because we so often do not experience sin as a wrong choice made with the options held before us evenly like "two roads diverg[ing] in a yellow wood." Rather, sin works as a compulsion, a force that does not feel like our own true will making the decision.[8]

Much modern psychology insists that human beings are subject to a panoply of controlling, or at least powerful, influences that drive our decisions, often unconsciously — ranging from internal influences including genetic dispositions to external forces such as social pressure and economic necessity. Paul might call these factors that dispose us toward sin "powers and principalities." Remember, Brian Nichols did not experience himself as exercising free will in his decision to kill. A few years ago, a pre-teen boy in an urban ghetto was invited by older boys to try crack. He refused, so they burned him alive. What kind of free will does such a child have?

The free will defense fits well in the worldview of modern democratic capitalism where the myth of freedom undergirds the way we organize our government and economy. However, the notion of free will is challenged from antiquity by Holy Scripture and from modernity by depth psychology, systems psychology, and behaviorism. In short, it is not as strong an argument as it seems at first glance.

As a response to the existential problem of evil, the one with the blood and tears, it does not work all that well. First, when people hurt us, we don't value their freedom so highly. Second, we often do not experience our own misdeeds as freely chosen. Finally, neither the perpetrators nor the victims of human evil always grow spiritually from the experience. In fact, the growth rate isn't very good.

Granted some freedom is a good thing. But how much freedom do we really need? Freedom obviously is not absolute. We live lives of limitation. We cannot do whatever we choose. Since free will is not absolute, we may ask whether people must have enough freedom to allow the worst forms of evil. If the possibility that someone may steal my car is the price I pay for a free and meaningful choice in human life, I'll gladly pay it many times over. If the possibility of someone killing my child is the price, that's another matter. Does a free and meaningful human life really require the possibility of what the Spanish did to the indigenous people of Latin America or what the Nazis did to Jews? Just how much freedom do we need to make life meaningful and interesting? Freedom may be sufficiently valuable to justify some level of evil, but it is not sufficient to justify the "horrendous evils" we encounter all too often.[9]

Finally, if free will is so absolute as to keep God always on the sidelines of life, then such a God is irrelevant to the things that really matter to us. This does not make for much of a God. As a line of graffiti in the restroom of the Hungarian Pastry Shop in New York City so aptly puts it, *"God isn't dead. He just doesn't want to get involved."*

DEMONS AND DUALISM

If "free will" is an explanation that may be too easily accepted in our time, there is another explanation that may be too readily rejected. It was the explanation that was more likely to be believed in antiquity. Whether it is right or not, blaming demonic powers is better than saying Brian Nichols was God's agent killing innocent people in a courthouse or that Judas was God's agent in killing Jesus. Remember the murdered judge's widow comparing Nichols to Judas and concluding they were both doing "God's will." Characterizing Judas as God's agent is not well supported by Scripture. In Matthew and Mark, Judas implicitly acts on the side of the demonic. Luke and John explicitly say that Judas was possessed by Satan.[10] In Scripture and most of Christian tradition, human evil is attributed to the influence of the demonic, not the divine.[11] James 1:13 insists God does not tempt people to do evil. But evil is not a pure free will choice by people either. There are dark forces at play to deprive people of their freedom and lead them into wrongdoing.

Such dark forces might be used to explain natural evil. Out of sheer malice, a malevolent force might visit us with disease, flood and famine. However, the demonic is mainly used to explain the perversity of human behavior. During the scientific 18th and 19th centuries, demonic powers ceased to be credible subjects for discussion. But the horrors of the 20th century led neo-orthodox theologians, including Paul Tillich, to take the demonic seriously once again. Individuals, groups, nations, and the world may sometimes fall under the sway of an influence from outside ourselves, an influence that leads us to do things beneath our true nature.[12]

The presence of demonic forces is to be taken seriously, though not necessarily in a literal sense.[13] There are undoubtedly forces beyond ourselves that ensnare us. Alcoholism, drug addiction, racism,

sexism, homophobia, classism, nationalism and other such forces impinge upon our free will in destructive ways. Family systems psychology shows that unconscious compulsions operate within groups driving people to behave in ways quite foreign to their natures. At a minimum, Satan makes an appropriate symbol for the multiple forces that oppress and corrupt creation.

For those who cannot relate to mythological imagery such as Satan, we will put the problem another way. Take the case of Karl. He is the elderly great uncle of a young cousin of mine. She is American. He is German. They met recently and he wanted to tell her as clearly as he could about his experience as a Nazi soldier. He explained how he had no choice but to work for Hitler. The force of Nazism was irresistible. So he fought for the Third Reich, but tried to do whatever kindnesses he could for the conquered and imprisoned. Karl was not completely free. He was compelled by the force of Nazism, the prime example of what theologian Paul Tillich meant by a demonic force. We can think of demonic forces as powers in the world, outside our own will, which force us to commit evil deeds. Such powers are not necessarily spooky or supernatural. But even

Photo: Remains of the victims of the Cambodian genocide under Pol Pot rule.
© Copyright LKEM. Some rights reserved. Used with permission.

so, where is God in this story? Did God create Nazism? Would a good God create such a force? Or is Nazism a manifestation of some eternal force at war with God? Let's see what we can learn from Scripture. The canonical Hebrew Scriptures do not know of any cosmic rival to God.[14] A God vs. Satan battle for the universe is not part of the Hebrew scripture's worldview.[15] In the New Testament, however, the demonic is a force to be reckoned with. Jesus is an exorcist.[16] Satan appears as a tempter in the wilderness. Paul exhorts Christians to resist "the principalities and powers of this present age," a term that refers both to political powers and spiritual forces. The New Testament clearly did not see God as running the world.[17] Rather the world is, as C. S. Lewis put it "in enemy hands." New Testament Christianity does not see the forces of evil as equal in power to God, but did posit that there are forces working against God's will and that they are running the affairs of the earth all too often for now.[18]

Christian tradition has regarded Satan as the tempter who leads us astray. The Baptismal Covenant of *The Book of Common Prayer*[19] calls upon those seeking baptism to "renounce Satan and all the spiritual forces of wickedness that rebel against God" and "the evil powers of this world which corrupt and destroy the creatures of God."

But how are we to make sense of the presence of demonic influence in a world created and ruled by a good God? Talking about demonic forces is only another way of poetically describing the problem of evil. It is not an answer. Did the good God create the evil Satan? Or is Satan co-eternal with God, so there are really two gods: one good and one bad? There is an old view, going back to Zoroastrianism, that we are morally neutral or at least highly impressionable. We are a battleground in a cosmic conflict between good and evil. To put Zoroastrian thought in Christian terms, some say God made us neutral and impressionable so we could serve as a prize to be fought over with his cosmic enemy, Satan. That scenario is also problematic. In that mythology, God's power is not only less than total, it is inadequate to assure or console.

The Christian view of God as the foundation of all reality won't allow for two gods. A full-fledged dualism won't work for us. If God is God, as we mean the word "God," then he has no equal. That leaves wide open the question of why there is evil in the world. That there are forces in the world opposed to God seems clear, but how did they get here?

It isn't necessary to create an archrival to God to explain why some things in creation are not as God would have them be. Former Archbishop of Canterbury Rowan Williams says God creates by allowing the existence of that which is not God. This view is more helpful. Since God allows the creation freedom, some parts of creation can cut off relationship with God or set themselves in opposition to God. We can posit the demonic existing without giving it equal status to God. The universe is truest to its nature when it loves its creator and engages in a relationship of reciprocity and mutual delight. But the universe is not under God's absolute control. It is free to love God or not. It is free to live in harmony or in discord. Milton gives us the classic story of the choice to reject God and live in discord.[20] In his epic *Paradise Lost*, the rejection of God gives rise to the demonic. So there is room for acknowledging that anti-God forces can exist in a world created by God if we accept that God allows the creation freedom. But that just leads us back where we started — to all the problems with the free-will defense.

ORIGINAL SIN AND LOSING THE GOOD

Augustine taught that God created all things and they are good. People are created in the image of God, which makes us especially good. God did not create evil because evil is not a thing. It is an absence of the good, a loss of the good. Augustine called sin and evil a deficit — the *privatio boni*, the privation or loss of the good. Death, for example, is not a thing, but the loss of a good thing, life.[21]

Regarding human misconduct, Augustine said at we are all motivated by love. Everything we do is driven by love, which in itself is good. The jewel thief steals for love of the jewel's beauty or of the good things he can buy with the money. He loves, which is good, and the object of his love is good. The jewels are good. The things he wants to buy are good. Even the worst acts are driven by love — but our love can be disordered, warped. The universal problem that afflicts all human beings is warped love. What then warps the love or "disorders our affections" to use his term? He says our affections are disordered by self-centeredness.[22]

Augustine is partly right. Death is an absence of life just as dark is an absence of light. We are sometimes like children who cry when the carousel ride is over — but if the carousel ride went on forever, there would be no joy in it. Still, his answers are far from satisfactory. They are more of a description than an explanation. Where did our self-centeredness come from? Saying all our other sins derive from a foundational sin does not explain the foundational sin. *Privatio boni* (privation of the good) does not explain who or what works the privation. It just brings us back to the question of why God made us mortal, vulnerable, finite and subject to "the thousand natural shocks that flesh is heir to."[23]

Calling evil a mere "privation of the good" is perilously close to denying it exists.[24] And it is not very helpful to us in coping with our actual suffering. A crippled spine may just be a straight spine disordered, but the pain and paralysis that ensue from that disorder cannot be lightly dismissed as "not a thing" but a mere privation. We experience our pain and our grief as quite real.

CONCLUSION

In Chapter 2, we considered explanations for things that go wrong in nature. We considered our mortal nature, natural law, and randomness. In this chapter, we have taken up explanations of the wrongs human beings perpetrate upon each other: free will, demons (bad influences from forces outside us), and Augustine's *privatio boni* (the notions that evil isn't a thing and sin is just love gone wrong). All of these explanations have some truth in them, truth that needs to be acknowledged if we are to look honestly at our human predicament. But none of them are satisfactory. They all leave us with a restless discomfort instead of hope and consolation. These explanations all assume a God who is either unwilling or unable to do us much good. In the next chapter, we will look at larger, comprehensive theories of why God causes or allows either natural or human evil. We will see if they are any better than what we have seen so far.

REFLECTION QUESTIONS

1. Do you see evil as just the loss of the good, or is there more to it? If so, what?

2. Do you believe there are forces outside the human will that tempt, influence or even compel bad behavior? Can you give examples? What name would you give to these forces? Where do you think they come from? Did God create them?

3. How much free will do you think people have? Are we all equally free? If people are not free, is it fair to hold us accountable for our actions?

4. What is your understanding of "original sin?" Does it seem true to you? If all of us are subject to the power of original sin, can we also have free will? Or does original sin only partly cut off our freedom?

5. Think of an evil person or an evil act. How do you explain why this person is as they are or why the act happened?

NOTES

1 Lyn Lifshin, "For Me the Holocaust Started in '33," in *The Blue Tattoo*.

2 Macon *Telegraph*, Vol. 180, Issue 70, p. 1A.

3 Harold Kushner, *When Bad Things Happen to Good People* (New York: Schockten Books, 1981), p. 81.

4 Alvin Plantinga, *God, Freedom, and Evil* (Grand Rapids: Wm. B. Eerdmans Publishing Co., 1974) pp. 29-34. Plantinga's "free will defense" is less ambitious in his view than Augustine's "free will theodicy." Plantinga merely purports to defend belief against the problem of evil by arguing that God might reasonably be all powerful and all good and yet permit evil in order to preserve the greater good if allowing freedom. Plantinga's argument differs from Augustine's "free Fall defense." For Plantinga, we

have to *remain* free individuals in order for the good of freedom to outweigh the evil we endure for its sake.

5 John Hick, *Evil and the God of Love* (New York: Harper and Row, 1978).

6 Michael Peterson, *God and Evil*, p. 41.

7 Romans 7:21-8:6.

8 Shirley Guthrie, *Christian Theology*, at 178.

9 Marilyn McCord Adams, *Horrendous Evils and the Goodness of God* (Ithaca: Cornell University Press, 1999).

10 Luke 22: 3; John 13: 27.

11 Making Judas and the executioners into God's agents is an understandable but wrong conclusion drawn from the tradition that Jesus submitted to crucifixion in obedience to God. Jesus' extraordinary, paradoxical response to evil is indeed an act of obedience. But the perpetrators of the evil are not obeying God.

12 "I speak of 'demons' as the actual spirituality of systems and structures that have betrayed their divine vocations. I use the expression "the Domination System" to indicate what happens when an entire network of Powers becomes integrated around idolatrous values. And I refer to 'Satan' as the world — encompassing spirit of the Domination System . . . I prefer to regard (demons) as impersonal realities at the center of institutional life." Walter Wink, *Engaging the Powers* (Minneapolis: Fortress Press, 1992), pp. 8-9. Wink's approach to the demonic closely follows that of Episcopal lawyer-theologian William Stringfellow.

13 "... (S)in is not to be equated with individual deeds, nor even the sum total of all history's sinful deeds. The evil which is unleashed in the world through the continuous distortion of human freedom acquires a life of its own. There are 'principalities and powers' which transcend the individual thoughts, words, and deeds through which they come to be enacted and are perpetuated." Douglas John Hall, *God and Human Suffering*, p. 87.

14 The term *ha-satan*, or Satan, refers simply to an obstacle, not a super-

natural opponent of God. The snake in Genesis is actually a snake, not Lucifer in scales or an agent of Beelzebub. The snake is actually a Semitic symbol of chaos. Joseph Kelly, *The Problem of Evil in the Western Tradition* (Collegeville: The Liturgical Press, 2002), p. 18. Satan shows up as a real player only in the story of Job, which isn't originally a Jewish story. It's a Moabite tale adapted to rebut the idea that misfortune only befalls the foolish and unrighteous. It isn't really intended to represent the Jewish view of God. Judaism would hardly imagine God frivolously playing with a human life over a bet with the devil. And in that story, it is really God that Satan tempts into doing wrong to a man, instead of tempting a man to betray God.

15   There is just a hint of an exception to this in 1 Chronicles 21: 1. This is the lone occasion in the Hebrew Scriptures in which Satan tempts a person to do wrong. This text, written in the Post-Exilic Era, perhaps even as late as after Alexander the Great's conquest, might be construed as showing Satan as an independent tempter. Even there, the role and motivation of Satan is entirely unclear. What's more the temptation is just to make a political mistake. Satan induces David to take a census. Granted, God was displeased — but it is not the sort of rebellion or tawdriness we might expect Satan to induce. Compare David's affair with Bathsheba and conspiracy to kill her husband in 1 Kings. That's considerably worse than a census, and Satan had nothing to do with it. David managed to create that mess on his own.

16   Joseph Kelley, *The Problem of Evil in the Western Tradition*, p. 33.

17   How this situation came about is not explained in Scripture, but early Christians adopted from Jewish apocalyptic literature a belief in fallen angels who rebel against God. Origen and Augustine identified pride as the cause of their fall. Joseph, Kelly, pp. 44, 53. Jewish apocalyptic literature had attributed the fall to angels' lusting after earthly women.

18   "(I)t is clearly the case that there is a 'provisional' dualism within the New Testament: not an ultimate dualism of course, between two equal principles; but certainly a conflict between a sphere of created autonomy that strives against God on the one hand and the saving love of God on the other. . . . For now, we live amid a strife of darkness and light, falsehood and truth, death and life." David Bentley Hart, *The Doors of the Sea: Where Was God in the Tsunami?* (Grand Rapids: Wm. B. Eerdmans Publishing Co., 2005), pp. 62-63, 66.

[19] The official worship book of the Episcopal Church, derived from *The Book of Common Prayer* adopted by the Church of England in 1662, and used as a supplemental worship text by various mainline Protestant denominations.

[20] Milton's use of rebellion imagery, inherited from Augustine who inherited it from Jewish apocalyptic literature, reflects the sense of God as dominator.

[21] While the doctrine of *privatio boni* is attributed to Augustine because he was such a giant in the history of theology, he did not invent the idea and he did not say the final word in articulating it. Clement of Alexandria argued that evil is not a thing but a privation of the good in the late 2nd century. And St. Anselm continued to develop that view in the 11th. Joseph Kelly, *The Problem of Evil in the Western Tradition* (Collegeville: The Liturgical Press, 2002), pp. 42, 53.

[22] Augustine's term was "concupiscence." "Concupiscence" today is equated with sexual desire. Augustine, in his own complicated and troubled relationship with sexuality, saw the problem as related to sex, in somewhat the same way that Freud saw everything as related to sex. But fundamentally, Augustine's concupiscence is not the sex drive. Our wrongdoing is only sometimes sexual. It is more often a matter of spite, greed, pride, jealously, envy and the like. Concupiscence has many forms. It is fundamentally self-indulgence, the attitude of "me first." It is the sense of self as separate from whatever is not-self, the aggressive tendency to advance self against others, the fear that makes us defensive. It corresponds more to the deadly sin of pride than to lust. The same confusion that attaches to Augustine's use of concupiscence attaches to Paul's use of *sarx*, traditionally translated as "flesh." But it does not mean sexuality or having a body. Paul uses *sarx* or flesh as a metaphor for ego; so some modern translations more accurately translate *sarx* as "self-indulgence."

[23] William Shakespeare, *Hamlet*.

[24] "The classical statement [denying or diminishing the reality of evil] is Augustine's account of evil as 'the privation of good'. He held that, just as darkness is not a positive quality but the absence of light, so evil is not a positive quality but the absence of goodness. In this century of suffering, this seems altogether too blithe a theory, failing to acknowledge the terrible intensity with which evil has been experienced." Polkinghorne, John. *Science and Theology*. (Minneapolis: Fortress Press, 1998), p. 93.

CHAPTER FOUR

'PERVERSE MOTIVES' ATTRIBUTED TO GOD FOR ALL MANNER OF SUFFERING

Any attempt to look upon suffering as caused directly or indirectly by God stands in danger of regarding him as sadistic.[1]
— Dorothee Soelle, *Suffering*

I was at home one night watching CNN when the anchor announced that TWA Flight 800 had just exploded on takeoff from New York City. Hour by hour through the night, more information came out, but the cause of the explosion remained unknown. The next morning I was praying in my office when I received a call from one of my friends: "Becky was on that plane." Becky was a twenty-year-old college student, always changing her major — art, anthropology, who knows what would have been next. She was fascinated by everything. Her long, wild, curly hair expressed pure *joi de vivre*. She was energetically zipping about being a feminist, blaming the patriarchy for all that was wrong in the world; she was a Taoist, who found nothing whatsoever wrong with the world; she was a warm, buoyant friend to an eclectic collection of artists, philosophy students, and poets. She was flying from New York to Paris for a backpacking jaunt through Europe with her good friend, also on the plane.

I hurried to her parents' home, where friends had gathered to wait for news from the search-and-rescue operation — a hopeless ordeal that only prolonged the agony. The moment I entered the house, I saw her mother's tears. She met me with the grief-choked question, "Why?" For months the crash went unexplained. Rumors flew. Terrorism. A missile fired by mistake from a navy submarine. No one could explain the disaster in terms of engineering, forensic science or politics. Eventually investigators settled on a small malfunctioning device that caused the fuel tank to explode. A glitch in the fuel system was so ludicrously petty in comparison to Becky's life. And there were many other lives lost, each as precious to someone as Becky was to us. A valve defect wasn't much of an answer. It said "how" but not "why."

Even Jesus cried from the cross: "Why have you forsaken me?" The explanations we give for suffering are not abstractions to test in a classroom. They are put to the test by real life and real death experience. So let's look at the answers that people have given to that question asked by Becky's mother — and by Jesus.

THE BIBLE TELLS ME SO

In chapter 2, we looked at theories about natural evil, the suffering wrought by disease, weather, genetic accidents, anything bad that happens without human intervention. In chapter 3, we investigated theories that apply to human evil, the wrongs we suffer at each other's hands. There are also comprehensive explanations that apply regardless of how suffering comes about. In this chapter, we will take up those broader theories that apply to hurricanes and terrorism alike. But first, we need to ask what the Bible says. We are in the midst of a hot debate over whether the Bible's answer makes sense. So we need to get clear on what the Bible has to say.

Bart Ehrman puts it most directly in saying "the Bible fails to answer" the problem of evil.[2] But the truth is the Bible doesn't even ask the question in the way Ehrman and others ask it today. As Ehrman admits, it was not until the 18th century that Scottish philosopher David Hume famously asked: "If God is omnipotent and perfectly good, then why is there evil in the world?"[3]

We may well wonder why the authors of the Bible were not dealing with Hume's logic puzzle. Ehrman says the problem has always been a pressing concern, noting that Hume cites the 4th-century BCE Greek philosopher Epicurus as asking the "problem of evil" question.[4] Hume, however, got Epicurus wrong. Epicurus was no Humean atheist. Like the rest of his society, Epicurus believed in a pantheon of gods, none of whom was omnipotent or necessarily good. His point was to deny that the gods cause suffering. He thought we caused our own suffering by needless fear of the gods, pain, and death. Hume believed in suffering, but not God; Epicurus believed in the gods, but not suffering — at least not as an inevitable part of existence. He thought suffering was mostly in our heads.[5]

Ehrman's mistake about the Bible parallels Hume's mistake about Epicurus. The Bible does not answer Hume's "problem of evil" question because Hume's image of God had not been invented yet; and without that image of God, the problem does not arise in the same intractable way.

The Jewish people did not begin as monotheists. The Hebrew Scriptures frequently refer to "the gods." The God of Israel was one of the gods, the one to whom Israel was bound in a sacred covenant. In the ancient world, the gods were understood to be often in conflict with each other. As time went by, the Jews came to see their god as the greatest of all the gods, eventually as the Lord or King of the other gods. Jewish monotheism was an accomplishment not easily achieved. The Babylonian Exile ended before Jewish monotheism took a clear shape in Third Isaiah. Even then, monotheism was less than fully developed.[6] The notion of one god as opposed to many gods did not yet redefine the word "God" into what we would later mean by that word. YHWH was a powerful supernatural person, but his jurisdiction was still largely focused on weather, war, politics, and fertility. His partner Wisdom oversaw the basic pattern of things in a manner something like natural law. But even together, they still do not comprise the image of God that was to emerge when Judaism met Hellenistic culture.

The Jewish God as we enter the New Testament era was anthropomorphic. He was a very big guy. The idea of God had not yet been infused with the "transcendent absolutes" of Platonic philosophy (Absolute Truth, Absolute Beauty, Absolute Goodness, Absolute Power). That process would not begin for Judaism until Philo of Alexandria in the 1st century CE, would not begin to influence Christian thought until Justin Martyr in the 2nd century, and would not come to fruition in Christianity until Augustine in the 4th century. Once that happened, the question about why there is evil in the world began to stir and Augustine offered the first comprehensive explanation, relying heavily on Plato and Plotinus, Greek philosophers, to make sense of a God who had now become an omnipotent Greek. A powerful Jewish God can rail and fight against evil; but an omnipotent Greek God ought to be able to just wish it away. His (more aptly Its) failure to do so called for an explanation. Besides, explaining things was a Greek sport. As Paul said, "While the Jews demand miracles and the Greeks look for wisdom, we are preaching a crucified Christ: to the

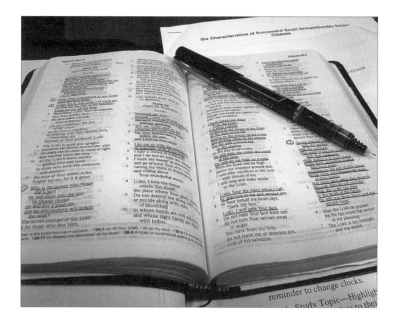

Jews an obstacle, to the gentiles foolishness."[7]

Even in Augustine's day, the question was why God did not stop evil. The idea that God caused evil was not yet being considered. The Christian notion of God would not be reshaped into Aristotle's "unmoved mover" who causes all things to happen (albeit indirectly) until Thomas Aquinas wrote the *Summa Theologica* in the High Middle Ages. The Aristotelian "mover" was to become the foundation for a God ultimately responsible for whatever happens — not that God was making bad things happen one by one — that idea was still 300 years way — but that God had set things in motion in a flawed or malicious way. This ultimate attribution of all events to God pushed Aquinas to adapt Augustine's arguments into a defense of God's choice to make the world as it is. Notably, Aquinas relied principally on Greek philosophical precedents, not the Bible, to make his case.[8] After Aquinas came centuries of conflict among European theologians over whether God's unfettered will or God's unchanging nature was dominant — that is, whether God's nature limits what God can do.

God's unfettered will won out in the 16th century when John Calvin defined God in terms of absolute "sovereignty." Not until

Photo: The Holy Bible / © Copyright George Bannister. Used with permission.

the next generation would Calvinists equate "sovereignty" with total dominance. God finally became the controller of everything, the puppet master of the universe. With that final shift, John Knox could impress the dominator God-image on the mind of Scotland, so that his fellow Scot, David Hume, could rightly say a century later, "This doesn't make sense."[9] The authors of the Bible had never heard of Knox's God, so they were not trying to defend him from Hume's question. The word "theodicy" — the defense of God's goodness in the face of the existence of evil — was coined in 1710 by Leibniz.[10] So we should not be surprised that the Bible does not contain "theodicy".

BIBLICAL COMPLAINTS ABOUT EVIL

The authors of the Bible did suffer and witness the suffering of others. They earnestly longed for their god to save them. Their god was not the absolutely good cause of everything; but he was their god, so they counted on him for protection. They prayed for it and complained bitterly when it did not happen. The logical problem of evil was not on their radar screen, but the existential experience of suffering decidedly was. Psalm 44 is a powerful protest that Israel had kept the covenant but God had, nonetheless, failed to deliver them from their enemies. This psalm rejects the notion that God sends suffering to punish sinners. The psalmist does not offer a theodicy, a defense of God's justice. As one scholar puts it, "The author [of Psalm 44] is trying to cope with suffering, not explain it."[11]

Psalm 44 does not explain suffering but does suggest a way to make meaning out of it. Verse 22 says, "For your sake we are being massacred." Psalm 69 likewise laments over "insults" endured "for (God's) sake." Scripture portrays the life of Jeremiah as one of suffering borne for fidelity to God.[12] The theme of suffering, not at God's hand as a punishment for sin, but rather at the world's hand as punishment for loyalty to God, continues in the Servant Songs of Second Isaiah.[13] These texts do not explain suffering but rather portray the sufferer as meaningfully heroic while continuing to hope that God will somehow, someday set things right.

While the logical problem of evil that drove Hume to deny God is a modern problem, the experience of suffering and the hope that God will deliver us from it are age-old. The Bible reflects those basic human struggles — but without giving a comprehensive theory of evil. Scripture offers many ideas and ultimately a vision of resurrection hope — but no neat explanation wrapped up in a tidy package with a bow on top. The Bible just isn't that kind of book. It is not a compendium of theological doctrines.

One respects Ehrman for his candid account of a spiritual struggle that led him to agnosticism. However, a biblical scholar knows and should acknowledge that the Bible is not an explanation book. Ehrman chides the Bible for "failing" to do something it does not attempt to do: explain things. The Bible is a sacred text containing a variety of kinds of literature. But there is not a single book of theology in it. As sacred text, the Bible provides the raw data for constructing doctrine. It does not provide the doctrine on its face.[14]

A philosophical explanation of evil would actually run flat contrary to the Bible's main attitude on the subject. An explanation would deny that evil is really evil and undermine resistance to it. Biblical faith doesn't undermine resistance. It undergirds resistance and the struggle to overcome all that falls short of the glory of God. As philosopher Marilyn McCord Adams observes, "The Bible is short on explanations of evil and relatively long on how God makes good on" the evils we endure.[15] Christians follow Jesus who died in protest, demanding the answer, "My God, my God, why have you forsaken me?" — not someone who offered a tidy explanation for why torture, oppression and injustice are really alright after all.

THEOLOGICAL ATTEMPTS TO EXPLAIN EVIL BASED ON SCRIPTURE

But the problem of evil, especially since medieval and Reformation theologians painted themselves into a corner, has been an impediment to faith. Since the 18th century, we have been trying especially hard to find ways to talk back to David Hume and to his modern proponents like John Mackie and Bart Ehrman. Some of the answers have been better than others, but none is satisfactory. They are all stuck in the dominator God-image, an image that precludes such answers from being very helpful. In this book, we are rethinking who God is by reclaiming ancient wisdom and integrating some of the best contemporary theology. But first we need to complete our survey of the efforts of our forebears to make sense of suffering. These are the theories that apply to all kinds of evil calamities that occur either naturally or at human hands.

> PUNISHMENT FOR OUR SINS
> I have no choice but to be guilty . . .
> Guilt matters. Guilt must always matter.
> Unless guilt matters the whole world is
> Meaningless. God too is nothing . . .
> I'd rather suffer
> Every unspeakable suffering God sends,
> Knowing it was I that suffered,
> I that earned the need to suffer,
> > I that acted, I that chose . . .
> > Can we be men
> > And make an irresponsible ignorance
> > Responsible for everything.[16]
> > — Archibald MacLeish, *J. B.* [J. B. speaking]

Ehrman cites multiple passages in scripture which portray suffering as a punishment for sins and demonstrates that such an idea does not make sense.[17] He is clearly right that such an interpretation of suffering flies in the face of our reason and experience. We see with our own eyes that affliction is both random and universal. It does not spare the good or particularly target the wicked. Do we seriously think the passengers on TWA 800 were, to a person, more sinful than the passengers on all the flights that land safely? Innocent babies are born with genetic handicaps. In old age, the righteous and the dissolute alike become diminished in their capacities, and we all die. In 2005, Hurricane Katrina devastated the Gulf Coast region of Alabama, Mississippi, and Louisiana. Recently, an Austrian pastor, who called Katrina "God's judgment" on sinful New Orleans, was promoted to bishop. Notably, God spared the French Quarter, but wiped out Slidell and Pascagoula. These facts called into question God's judgment or at least God's aim.

Does the Bible, however, actually insist that Christians equate affliction with punishment? Granted, the texts cited by Ehrman are part of scripture. But to be fair, we need to consider three major qualifications. First, a host of Biblical texts explicitly reject the idea that suffering can be explained or justified this way. It is by and large the earlier writings that treat blessing and affliction as carrots and sticks to make people more moral. Israel outgrew the view that God rewards good people with earthly flourishing and punishes bad people with misfortune. The authors of the later Hebrew scriptures saw that good people often suffered while scoundrels flourished. They saw that their earlier carrot-and-stick theology was wrong. The Bible is a history of evolving beliefs. Later texts suggest other ways to think of calamities. We have previously discussed heroic suffering in Second Isaiah.[18] Ecclesiastes, traditionally attributed to Solomon, reads more as if it were written by Epicurus with a hangover. Life is just meaningless. But that viewpoint is explicitly repudiated in the Book of Wisdom. Job — ah, Job — can be read in such different ways. It may be read as a "test of faith" or "spiritual exercise" story in which Job learns to love God for God's own sake, not for what God does for him[19]; as a story of doubt that says God is powerful but unjust like the heartless universe[20]; or as a story of love leading to liberation.[21] The Bible does not explain suffering. But the notion of suffering as divine retribution was repudiated by most of the later authors of scripture.

If we read the whole Bible, rather than focusing just on the older verses, the Hebrew scriptures do not teach that God punishes sin with adversity. Jesus explicitly repudiated that idea. He said that God causes the rain to fall and the sun to shine on the just and the unjust alike.[22]

The second qualification is to put those early biblical passages in the context of Antiquity. Most ancient peoples, not just Jews, regarded affliction and flourishing as expressions of the favor or disfavor of the gods, who caused disease and famine or granted health and fertility. Most ancient religion practiced sacrifices to appease the deities and win their favor. Religion was an elaborate system of bribery and cosmic graft.

The 8th-century prophets Ehrman chides shifted Judaism to link God's favor to morality instead of bribery. The prophets were not trying to answer the "problem of evil." They were saying God cares about justice, not cultic observance. We cannot accept this carrot and stick religion, but it made sense in the context of the ancient worldview, and was in fact an admirable advance in religion.

Third, the texts that link sin and suffering convey a universal human sense of justice, expressed from the Vedic scriptures to contemporary action movies. The bad guys *ought* to get their comeuppance. It is this sense of justice that makes us ask the problem of evil question.[23]

Although the Hebrew scriptures and Jesus rejected the "divine retribution" theory, it cropped back up in Christianity through a distortion of the teaching that God is just. Some Christians conceive of God's justice as an algebra equation of crime and punishment. Each quantity of sin must be balanced by an equal quantity of retribution. So they claim that God inflicts suffering as divine retribution. Such spirituality of groveling in fear is disturbingly masochistic. This prayer by John Calvin is a prime example:

> And surely, O Lord, from the very chastisements which thou hast inflicted upon us, we know that for the justest causes thy wrath is kindled against us; for, seeing thou art a just Judge, thou afflictest not thy people when not offending. Therefore, beaten with thy stripes, we acknowledge that we have provoked thy anger against us; and even now see thy hand stretched forth for our punishment.[24]

The idea that God needs so desperately to see crime punished deifies our own obsession with vengeance. It fans the flames of our own vengeful inclinations. It girds them with a claim of godliness. Worshipers of a vengeful God become vengeful. No one is more violent than those who fancy themselves as avenging angels. In *The Hour I First Believed*, Wally Lamb's novel about the Columbine High School murders, one of the teenage killers says, "My wrath will be God-like."[25]

The biblical concept of justice, however, is not an algebraic equation of crime and punishment. It isn't about wrath and retribution but rather, right relationships. The Hebrew word translated as "righteousness" and interpreted as "justice" is *sedeq*, which really means keeping promises in covenant. Biblical *sedeq* is faithfulness: God's faithfulness to Israel, Israel's faithfulness to God, people's faithfulness to each other. The *sedeq* of God is about God showing up for people who need saving — quite a different matter from an obsession with vengeance. Biblical *sedeq* will not support an understanding of suffering as required by God's justice. The biblical concept of God's justice as preserving and restoring relationships does not explain evil; it provides a ground for hope. God's justice sets things right and heals our broken lives and relationships.[26]

We have already said that equating affliction with punishment doesn't fit the facts. It isn't credible. The theological implications of that idea are even worse. Claiming that God punishes sin with earthly misfortune portrays God as a tyrant enforcing his will with the lash, and often using the cruelest of sinners as his agents. This is precisely the religion that plants bombs in women's clinics and on commuter trains. Theologian Dorothee Soelle calls this approach "theological sadism": "The ultimate conclusion of theological sadism is worshiping the executioner."[27]

But lest we throw the baby out with the bath, let's consider that there may be some truth in this generally bad theology. Sin and suffering are actually sometimes connected — just not as crime and punishment. Sin often takes the form of social injustice that hurts people. It causes us to wound and afflict each other.[28] For example, the sin of racism twists society, poisoning relationships and misshaping attitudes. The inheritance of sins such as slavery and segregation still hurt people today. In that sense, sin causes suffering, diminishing the lives of all races and classes of people. Think of the wounds inflicted by alcoholism, drug addiction, and family violence — wounds that scar generation after generation. In that sense, sin causes suffering. But crime and punishment is a poor analogy for sin and suffering. The analogy of disease and symptom is more apt.

TESTS OF FAITH AND SPIRITUAL GROWTH
Every human creature born
Is born into the bright delusion
Beauty and loving-kindness care for him.
Suffering teaches! Suffering is good for us!
Imagine men and women dying
Still believing that the cuddling arms
Enclosed them! . . .
We learn to wish we'd never lived.[29]
    — Archibald MacLeish, *J. B.* [Nickles speaking]

"Affliction as punishment" does not carry much weight among today's theologians. Saddling contemporary Christianity with that notion is truly not fair. But some of our best minds are inclined to interpret hardship as an opportunity for spiritual growth. Suffering can be understood as a test or an exercise. This approach is better because it attributes tough love, instead of vengeance, to God. But it is still problematic.

Let's begin with the "test of faith" view before dealing with the closely related "spiritual exercise" theory. "Test of faith" regards affliction as a kind of trial or temptation to measure the degree of faith the sufferer has developed. The story of Job can be read this way, and

I Peter 1:6-9 supports that view.[30] The problem with "test of faith" is that it posits a seriously flawed view of God. Just ask: How do we feel about the cosmic proctor administering a moral midterm? Louise Glück protests against that kind of God in her poem "Matins (3)":

What is my heart to you
that you must break it over and over
like a plantsman testing
his new species? [31]

It is hard to worship and adore someone who would give us cancer to see how we handle it. Besides, this theory just doesn't fit with the rest of what we believe about God. Does God test our characters with broken relationships, diseases, and social injustice? The notion is patently absurd. Scripture is quite clear that God knows us quite well already:

Lord you have searched me out and known me;
  you know my sitting down and my rising up;
  you discern my thoughts from afar.
You trace my journeys and my resting places
  and are acquainted with all my ways.
Indeed there is not a word on my lips
  but you O Lord know it altogether.
         — Psalm 139:1-4

One of the Church's prayers begins, "Almighty God, unto whom all hearts are open, from whom no secrets are hid." God doesn't need to administer tests. The tragedies that we are calling "tests" are the sorts of tests that might be dreamed up by Joseph Mengele. The God of Christianity does not afflict us out of curiosity to see how we'll respond. Louise Glück protested against the God of the inhuman experiment, the God who "tests our faith." Then she quickly saw that the God against whom she rebelled was a straw man, not the true God. In "Matins (4)," she writes:

I am ashamed
at what I thought you were,
  distant from us, regarding us
  as an experiment: it is

a bitter thing to be
the disposable animal,
a bitter thing. Dear friend,
dear trembling partner, what
surprises you most in what you feel,
earth's radiance or your own delight?[32]

The only way to read the "test of faith" idea as saying something worthy of consideration is to interpret the "test" not as an examination, but as an exercise in faith. That idea has been embraced by notable theologians such as Simone Weil, Diogenes Allen, D. Z. Phillips, and John Hick. They have offered truly compelling arguments that God has designed the world as a spiritual boot camp to whip us into shape.

The Christian tradition is not alone in its claim that suffering can humanize us and make us wise. Aeschylus and Sophocles rarely wrote a play that did not include the line "I have suffered into truth." Undoubtedly, the idea of suffering as a way to grow spiritually has deep roots in the Christian tradition, too. St. Paul said, "I want to share in the sufferings of Christ . . . if I may somehow attain the resurrection from the dead." St. Ireneaus, in the 3rd century, taught that evil was in the world in order to help us to grow toward holiness.[33] The Book of Hebrews opines that "God disciplines those he loves" and that "all discipline is painful" (but not that all pain is discipline). In the 14th century, Lady Julian of Norwich prayed for the wounds of true contrition, true longing for God, and a serious illness to purify her soul. In her classic *Shewings*, she said the wounds of life lead to greater honor and joy than we could experience without them.[34]

We must acknowledge that suffering and spiritual growth are sometimes, at least potentially, connected. In the Christian tradition, there are two versions of the idea that suffering is good for us. A view that D. Z. Phillips calls the "Outward Bound" school of theology holds that our own suffering poses challenges that enable us to develop heroic virtues, and the suffering of others gives us opportunities to practice mercy.[35]

I call the other theory the *Casablanca* school of theology ("the problems of three little people don't amount to a hill of beans in this crazy world").[36] The Casablanca school does not see God as sending specific sufferings, but as leaving the universe to function unrestrained and therefore with amoral indifference to our well being. From the resulting hardships, we should learn that we are insignificant. This insight liberates us from our egos.

Both views have some merit, but I cannot unqualifiedly accept either of them. As with the "divine retribution theory," this "spiritual growth" theodicy is undercut by the facts we experience. So much suffering is grinding, dehumanizing and embittering. Suffering is as likely to disintegrate us as it is to ennoble us.

Does this theology offer a God we can worship and adore? No. It reduces God to a cosmic drill sergeant. Such a God-image may be more benign than the cosmic executioner, who punishes us for our moral lapses, but it is still a small-hearted God, using carrots and sticks to enforce his will. It is hard, and perhaps not healthy, to love such a God. His character still smacks of sadism.

So how shall we sort out the truth from the falsehood in this approach to suffering? It is crucial here to distinguish a *cause* from a *purpose*, and a *purpose* from a *justification*.[37] Spiritual growth will not do as a cause of suffering. God doesn't send affliction like a thunderbolt to humble us. But our choice to use our suffering as an occasion for growth is another matter. Purpose and meaning are not just lying there before the event in an objective way for us to discover. Purpose and meaning are fashioned by our own interpretation and actions. Suffering and grief are sometimes somewhat redeemed from utter meaninglessness by spiritual transformation. Suffering isn't caused by our need to grow, but we can grow through suffering and so give it a purpose or meaning.

The possibility of making productive spiritual use of our suffering still doesn't *justify* what happened to us. That would be a false defense of evil and injustice. Simone Weil, of all people, a brave fighter against fascism, certainly never intended that. Rabbi Harold Kushner described what he had gained spiritually from the death of his son Aaron, but acknowledged the gains did not justify the loss:

I am a more sensitive person, a more effective pastor, a more sympathetic counselor because of Aaron's life and death than I would ever have been without it. And I would give up all those gains in a second if I could have my son back. If I could choose, I would forego all the spiritual growth and depth. . . and become what I was fifteen years ago, an indifferent counselor, . . . and the father of a bright, happy boy. But I cannot choose.[38]

Spiritual growth does not justify our suffering. But it can often paint the silver lining. If Kushner had shriveled into bitterness when his son died, he would have suffered just as much, perhaps more, but without finding any meaning or value in it. In fact, it would have made the meaning of his son's death even worse. Kushner says:

> We, by our responses, give suffering either a positive or a negative meaning. Illnesses, accidents, human tragedies kill people. But they do not necessarily kill life or faith. If the death and suffering of someone we love makes us bitter, jealous, against all religion, and incapable of happiness, we turn the person who died into one of the "devil's martyrs." If suffering and death in someone close to us bring us to explore the limits of our capacity for strength and love and cheerfulness, if it leads us to discover sources of consolation we never knew before, then we make the person into a witness for the affirmation of life rather than its rejection.[39]

It is not always possible to turn pain into wisdom and compassion, but when it is possible, it is a profound way to live through affliction. Making meaning is a spiritual challenge life sets for us. We grow stronger in the process of trying to meet it. The irony in Archibald MacLeish's *J. B.* is this: The "God" character is an immoral tyrant who subjects J. B. to unendurable suffering just to win a bet. But J. B. makes meaning of his suffering in the end, by resolving to love in spite of it all, knowing that love entails suffering, but that same love makes life worthwhile anyway.

PROVIDENCE: GOD'S SECRET PLAN

The doctrine of providence is another widely held response to the problem of evil. This doctrine holds that God is actively involved in the world to move it toward a holy and noble purpose that is beyond our comprehension. In this view, seeming catastrophes serve a good purpose in God's secret plan. In contrast to the idea that the world runs according to "free process," the doctrine of providence asserts that God's hand is at work, moving for a mysterious good. Nothing bad actually happens. It just looks bad to us in the short run.

Providence is a much larger doctrine than we are considering here. It is at the core of Calvinism and a profound insight into how God's grace heals and redeems our lives. This chapter is not meant to evaluate the doctrine as a whole, only the aspect of it that is used as an explanation for seemingly senseless suffering. For example, one day a tornado flattened a credit union in a city near mine. The next day, my bank teller mentioned this, then said, "But it's for a purpose." Was it? Is each tornado on a clandestine divine mission? Does God have a secret motive for demolishing a credit union in a small town in Georgia?

The randomness of misfortune calls providence into question. Even theologians who defend the Calvinist view of providence now make some allowance for randomness. John Macquarrie, for example, acknowledges, "If creation is [an] open, unfinished process . . . , one would expect to find evidences of untidiness and loose ends, of chance and necessity, alongside whatever one might discern of purpose."[40] Macquarrie grants some random chance to be at work, but he regards it as a "loose end," not part of God's plan. John Polkinghorne sees the looseness of most ends as precisely what God has in mind, at least for now.[41] It would seem hard, in any specific case, to sort out whether this particular catastrophe was a loose end or a case of suffering for a greater good yet to be revealed.

Providence is a fine doctrine to explain our experiences of God's love and mercy. It is not so helpful in explaining evil. First, it "attributes perverse motives to God."[42] Second, when it says there is a secret reason we cannot know, it shuts down our minds instead of opening them to deeper understanding. Third, it denies that evil is really evil. It makes all manner of evil—the crash of TWA 800, the Rwandan genocide, human trafficking, serial killers, the HIV/AIDS epidemic — all good things. We are just too ignorant to understand why they are good.

Providence, used to defend evil, is not in line with the ancient stance of Judaism, Christianity, and Islam. It is actually more in line with the Vedic tradition of ancient India, which went to great lengths to explain suffering. The Vedantists didn't attribute suffering to their gods, as the Greek pagans did. But they did have two ways of taking unjust and arbitrary affliction out of the picture. One was to say (with Epicurus) suffering was simply an illusion, a trick of the mind; we just need to see through the illusion. The other option is to say the affliction is perfectly just and part of a larger picture of harmony. The seeming injustice and randomness of pain can be explained away by the laws of karma, which justify seemingly outrageous situations. This is an attitude closely akin to belief in providence. Things only seem to be "out of joint." Everything is actually alright.

"We all get what we deserve," the Vedantists said. When disasters befell folks who obviously did not deserve them, Vedic philosophers said it was punishment for what these innocent people had done in another life. The moral order of the universe, they insisted, was perfectly balanced. The poor deserved to be poor, the sick deserved to be sick, those imprisoned and tortured deserved what they got. By their reasoning, Africans deserved slavery, Native Americans deserved to be massacred, and Jews deserved to be exterminated by Hitler.

The world's religions, especially those arising out of the Vedic tradition, are a wealth of wisdom. But no religion is exempt from reasoned critique. Religions that deny the existence of suffering and injustice, or that defend and justify them, perpetuate misery, foster a sense of personal powerlessness, and instill masochistic passivity in the face of misery and oppression. Religions that call AIDS God's judgment will not inspire the quest for a cure; religions that treat oppression as divinely ordained will not produce liberation movements. Dominique Lapierre's novel *The City of Joy*[43] is an excellent portrait of the passivity instilled by fatalistic religion. In Lapierre's story, a western doctor finds solace in the wisdom of the East, but also inspires oppressed people in India to demand justice.

Robert Browning perhaps mocked the Christian version of such passive religion in "Pippa's Song," his poem about a little orphan girl witnessing all sorts of human misery but going on blithely singing, "God's in His heaven; all's right with the world."[44] Christianity is every bit as problematic as Vedic religion when it says, "It's all God's will. So just accept what comes." Such religion relieves us of the question "Why?" by shrugging, "That's just how it is." It worships the God of the way things are, not the God of infinite possibilities. That kind of religion sanctions suffering and injustice.

There is a popular New Age variation on this kind of religion that goes, "Suffering is caused by our own negative thinking." It's an echo of Epicurus. In Christian parlance, it comes out, "If you only have enough faith, it will be alright." That view teaches that if we simply keep the right attitude, all will go well for our health, wealth, and social life. Conversely, if one is sick, poor or lonely, those conditions reveal the sufferer's spiritual inadequacy. Douglas John Hall opines,

"The world fairly hums with the speculations of those who would demonstrate that suffering is unreal, temporary, illusory, a mere cultural lag, technologically containable, progressively being overcome, a figment of the imagination, etc."[45] The Book of Job was included in the Hebrew scriptures to repudiate such blame-the-victim theology. Pious fatalism sometimes seems to console some people. But as a generalized doctrine, it is insidious whether it goes by the name of karma or providence.

FROM EXCUSES TO HOPE

The doctrines we have considered were not made up lightly by academic dilettantes sitting on salon couches. They are serious attempts by serious people to struggle with the most serious of questions. They are the struggles of brilliant theologians striving to answer the anguished "Why?" sometimes asked in their own hearts, flailing desperately to come to terms with their own grief. They deserve our respect. Most of these explanations contain a valuable measure of truth.

Cumulatively, these doctrines offer us a complex explanation of adversity. Evil and affliction are not only complex; they are mysterious. There is no one, final answer that sweepingly explains all forms of adversity. So what are we to do with the remaining anguish? We have a choice to make. We can side with Hume, Mackie and Ehrman. We can reject God — but that rejection does not solve anything. It does not console, sustain, empower or inspire. Moreover, if we take God out of the equation, we still have not explained suffering.

The other option is to trust the mystery. We might trust that God acts and permits for reasons, but because God is an infinite mystery, we cannot fully comprehend God's motives. This appeal to mystery, however, does not complete our answer; it only acknowledges our failure. We have not explained evil in a way that provides meaning or purpose to those who endure it.

These explanations do not satisfy because *explanations* are not the kind of answer we need. The "Why?" exclaimed by afflicted people is the cry of Jesus on the Cross: "My God, my God, why have you forsaken me?" Explaining to Jesus that he is just experiencing his mortal nature, or that crucifixion is actually just a "privation of the good," or that Pilate needs free will so his life can be meaningful will not help much. We need some response to the pain, a response that consoles, sustains, and empowers — not a response that sugarcoats the truth, not a response that tells us the injustice and misfortune we see are alright after all. In truth, when Jesus cries out, he does not want a memo of explanation. He wants his Father to show up and do something.

The emptiness of such explanations was central to Karl Marx's famous attack on religion as "the opiate of the masses."[46] Marx regarded theodicies as prescriptions for docility in the face of oppression, as his epitaph argues: "The philosophers wanted to understand the world, but the point is to change it." Marx critiqued the various forms of religion for naive optimism, fatalistic pessimism, and escapist separation from the world — all bulwarks for the current power structure. He was, however, disregarding the prophetic tradition of Amos, Hosea and Joel, which liberation theologians reclaimed. Some have even considered Marx a secularized voice of that tradition.

Marx is joined by many secular activists and existentialists in attacking religion for explaining suffering; yet, others have faulted religion for failing to explain it. Which is it? Christian faith, at its best, does not purport to defend the misery in the status quo. If we did so, if we provided the kind of answer Ehrman demands, we would be precisely the "opiate" Marx said we are. Biblical theologian J. Chritiaan Becker argues that the Bible offers a variety of understandings of suffering. Some suffering is meaningful; other suffering is tragically meaningless. Some suffering is unjust, inflicted by oppressors; other suffering is part and parcel of the human condition. The biblical responses to these different forms of suffering are different. The overarching theme of the Bible, the unifying message, is not an explanation for suffering, certainly not a defense of it. The Bible acknowledges that suffering is real but it also insists that there is hope.[47]

The most authentic Christian tradition (along with Judaism and Islam) faces the pain straight on and says, "This should not be." The biblical tradition includes the prophets' protest against the injustice of kings; the psalms of lament over suffering and loss; the history of fights for liberation; the record of longing for a messiah, a return of Christ in glory, the coming of a kingdom in which God's will is finally done on earth as it is in heaven. If the world already ran according to God's will, Jesus would not have taught us to pray "Thy will be done, thy kingdom come."

'PERVERSE MOTIVES' ATTRIBUTED TO GOD FOR ALL MANNER OF SUFFERING

Theologian Nicholas Wolterstorff, in his intimately personal reflection *Lament for a Son*, is true to this tradition when he offers this advice to those who would console a grieving parent with platitudes explaining death:

Don't say it's really not so bad. Because it is. Death is awful, demonic. If you think your task as a comforter is to tell me that really, all things considered, it's not so bad, you do not sit with me but place yourself off in the distance away from me. . . . I know: people sometimes think things are more awful than they are. Such people need to be corrected—gently, eventually. But no one thinks death is more awful than it is. It's those who think it's not so bad that need correcting.[48]

Wolterstorff will brook no pious opiates. He echoes the sentiments of Sarah in *J. B.* She has heard her husband and others expound upon the various theodicies to justify the deaths of her children. But she will not be consoled. It is not just that she is unpersuaded as a matter of cold logic. She is unwilling to conscience any justification for death:

Dead! And they were innocent!
I will not
Let you sacrifice their deaths
To make injustice justice and God good!
Must we buy quiet with their innocence —
Theirs and yours?
I cannot stay here —
I cannot stay here if you cringe
Connive in death's injustice, kneel to it —
Not if you betray my children.[49]

Ivan Karamazov would say a reverent amen to her protest. So would the Jewish, Christian and Islamic traditions at their best. These religious traditions side with Wolterstorff, Sarah and Ivan in that they lay the groundwork for dealing boldly and creatively with affliction and injustice, first by acknowledging they exist but should not; and second, by hoping to move beyond them.[50] We lay the groundwork for engaging suffering by admitting it's there, but refusing to accept it as inevitable or permanent.

The price we pay for that groundwork is coming face to face with the thorny problem of evil. If we cannot find anything at all helpful to say in the face of affliction, then we leave the world disconsolate. But if we answer the problem too satisfactorily, we become a religion of the status quo by justifying evil instead of resisting and overcoming it. Conservative scholar N. T. Wright says:

[T]here is a noble Christian tradition which takes evil so seriously that it warns against the temptation to "solve" it in any obvious way. If you offer an analysis of evil, saying "Well that's alright then; we see how it happens and we know what to do about it," you have belittled the problem. . . . We must not soften the blow; we cannot and must not pretend that evil is not so bad after all.[51]

Instead, we hope for a religion that inspires and empowers people to live through and overcome their own losses and to regard the suffering of others with compassion, not pious gloating. If we are to have that kind of religion, we must insist that God is by no means the explanation or justification for our affliction. God is the ground upon which we stand to protest against injustice and affliction. As liberation theologian Jurgen Moltmann says:

If it were not for their desire for life, the living would not suffer. If there were no love of justice, there would be no rebellion against innocent suffering . . . . If there were no God, the world would be alright. It is only the desire, the passion, the thirst for God which turns suffering into conscious pain and turns the consciousness of pain into protest against suffering.[52]

So if God is not an explanation or justification for calamity, injustice and affliction, who is God? We need a different sort of God, a better God, a God who deserves our worship and adoration. We need a God who is the ground on which we stand to protest injustice and respond to misery with compassion.

We now turn from the causes of suffering to how God responds to it. As we have repudiated the inadequate explanations of evil in the first three chapters, we must now, in the next chapters, repudiate the inadequate concepts of God that are woven into them. We must cast aside the God of the way things are in order to see the God of infinite possibilities, the God of hope who saves.

CONCLUSION

First, we considered the causes for natural evil (mortal nature, natural law, and randomness); then when we considered the explanations for human evil (free will, demonic influences, love gone wrong); the answers were all a bit true. They were partial answers but as Marilyn McCord Adams says, when we try to blow a little truth up into a big theory, it doesn't work and it "attributes perverse motives to God."

Now, when we try to sum up all the bad things with sweeping generalized explanations, and when we try invoking a complex book like the Bible — which actually says many things — as if it said one thing, to support our sweeping theories, the answers are even less satisfactory. Punishment for sin, test of faith and spiritual growth, and divine providence portray a particularly perverse God and fail all the more to comfort or encourage.

A better reading of the Bible and the insights of theologians and scholars such as Becker, Hall, Wolterstorff, Wright and Moltmann affirm that Christian faith does not rest on any of the explanations of evil we have considered. It rests on a God who redeems us from suffering rather than afflicting us, who heals our wounds rather than inflicting them on us. From here forward, we will be looking for that God. But first we have to clear the way. We have to repudiate false teachings about God that have made the problem of evil "the rock of atheism" and have trapped our religious imaginations in these inadequate answers.

We now turn our attention to recovering the older, richer, truer sense of the God who will sustain and empower us in a hard world. We are seeking the God described by James Weldon Johnson:

God of our weary years,
  God of our silent tears,
  Thou who hast brought us thus far on the way;
  Thou who hast by thy might,
  Led us into the light,
  Keep us forever on the path, we pray.[53]

REFLECTION QUESTIONS

1. Have you known people who have suffered and grown wise and compassionate through their suffering? Have you known people who have been spiritually crippled by suffering, or made cynical or hard-hearted? What made the difference in their personal stories? Did the difference lie in the nature of the affliction or in the person who suffered? Again, this is not a rhetorical question. Think carefully and be honest.

2. Have you ever felt that God was punishing you? What happened to make you think you were being punished? Did this thought give you hope that you could escape future punishment by repentance and good behavior?

3. Do you believe God has a plan for humanity? If so, does this plan include our suffering? Or is suffering part of God's Plan B, that is, God didn't intend for us to suffer, but he has a way to weave suffering into his plan to make something good of it? Or is our suffering just plain contrary to God's will?

4. The genocide of European Jews in the mid-20th century has traditionally been called the "Holocaust," a term that refers to a burnt offering sacrifice. More recently, many Jews have objected to the use of a term that suggests meaning and value in Hitler's atrocities, and have chosen to refer to that historic tragedy as the *shoah*, or catastrophe. Do you see more value in thinking of atrocities as sacrifices or catastrophes?

5. What do you think of Karl Marx's criticism of the whole project of explaining suffering and finding meaning in it? Do philosophy and religion justify oppression and take the edge off our desire to make things better? What do you think of the two defenses sometimes offered in reply to Marx: some suffering is inevitable, and even suffering that can be overcome must first be understood?

6. If we do not explain and justify suffering, is there anything we can say in the face of human misery that might in any way be helpful?

NOTES

1 Dorothee Soelle, *Suffering*, trans. Everett Kalin (Philadelphia: Fortress Press, 1975), p. 25.

2 Bart Ehrman, *God's Problem: How the Bible Fails to Answer Our Most Important Question—Why We Suffer* (New York: HarperCollins, 2008).

3 Ibid., p. 10.

4 Ibid. Epicurus thought the crocodile's existence disproved any notion that the gods had created the world.

5 Jennifer Michael Hecht, *Doubt: A History* (New York: HarperOne, 2003), pp. 34-41. Epicurus is not so much a precursor of Hume as of the 17th-century Dutch philosopher Spinoza and of Christian Science teachings. Spinoza and Mary Baker Eddy denied the existence of evil and claimed our experience of evil was just a poor understanding of the big picture. John Hick, *Evil and the God of Love* (London: Palgrave MacMillan, 1966), pp. 17-25.

6 Miguel de Unamuno, *The Tragic Sense of Life in Men and Nations*, trans. Anthony Kerrigan (Princeton, NJ: Princeton University Press, 1972), p. 67.

7 1 Corinthians 1: pp. 22-23.

8 Hick, *Evil and the God of Love*, pp. 93-98.

9 The dominator image of God raised the concern of God's responsibility to heightened levels in the generations immediately preceding Hume. Anglican Archbishop William King and John Clarke in England and Gottfried Leibniz in Germany addressed the issue with an idea then known as "optimism," holding that God had really given us as good a world as he could. These arguments sparked Voltaire to challenge their optimistic view of God with satire. Hume followed suit with logic (Hick, *Evil and the God of Love*, pp. 145-46).

10 Leibniz wrote his theodicy to refute Bayle, a precursor of Hume. Susan Nieman, *Evil in Modern Thought* (Princeton: Princeton University Press, 2002), pp. 14-31.

[11] George Martin, "Psalm 44: Suffering 'For The Sake Of God,'" in *The Bible on Suffering: Social and Political Implications*, ed. Anthony J. Tambasco (New York: Paulist Press, 2001), p. 21.

[12] Ibid., pp. 24—31.

[13] Carol J. Dempsey and Anthony J. Tambasco, "Isaiah 52: 13—53: 12: Unmasking the Mystery of the Suffering Servant," in Tambasco, *The Bible on Suffering*, pp. 34-49.

[14] N. T. Wright, *Evil and the Justice of God* (Downers Grove, IL: InterVarsity Press, 2006), pp. 40-41, 45, 93.

[15] Marilyn McCord Adams, *Horrendous Evils and the Goodness of God* (Ithaca, NY: Cornell University Press, 1999), p. 137.

[16] Archibald MacLeish, *J. B.: A Play in Verse* (Boston: Houghton Mifflin, 1956), pp. 110, 121, 123.

[17] Ehrman, *God's Problem*, pp. 21-123.

[18] Dempsey and Tambasco, "Isaiah," pp. 34-49.

[19] Susan F. Matthews, "All for Naught: My Servant Job," in Tambasco, *The Bible on Suffering*, pp. 51-69.

[20] Hecht, *Doubt*, pp. 62-74.

[21] Gustavo Gutierrez, *On Job: God-Talk and Suffering of the Innocent* (Maryknoll, NY: Orbis Books, 1985).

[22] Luke 13: 2—5; Matthew 5: 45; David Kelsey, *Imagining Redemption* (Louisville, KY: Westminster John Knox Press, 2005), pp. 47-51.

[23] Susan Nieman, *Evil in Modern Thought,* (citing Kant).

[24] John Calvin, "Forms of Prayer for the Church," in *Tracts and Treatises on the Doctrine and Worship of the Church*, trans. Henry Beveridge, vol. 2 (Grand Rapids, MI: Eerdmans, 1958), 108ff, quoted in Soelle, *Suffering,* p. 9. While Calvin's prayer sounds egregious to modern ears, he did not invent

this belief out of whole cloth. It is an extension of the medieval theology and piety that regarded suffering as the wrath of God.

25 Wally Lamb, *The Hour I First Believed* (New York: HarperCollins, 2008), p. 3.

26 "God's justice is not simply a blind dispensing of rewards to the virtuous and punishments for the wicked. . . . God's justice is a healing, saving, restorative justice" (Wright, *Evil and the Justice of God*, p. 64).

27 Soelle, *Suffering*, p. 25.

28 Douglas John Hall, *God and Human Suffering* (Minneapolis, MN: Augsburg Publishing House, 1986), pp. 82-89.

29 MacLeish, *J. B.*, p. 49.

30 "In this you rejoice, even if now for a little while you have had to suffer various trials, so that the genuineness of your faith — being more precious than gold that, though perishable, is tested by fire — may be found to result in praise and glory and honor when Jesus Christ is revealed. Although you have not seen him, you love him; and even though you do not see him now, you believe in him and rejoice with an indescribable and glorious joy, for you are receiving the outcome of your faith, the salvation of your souls." The treatment of suffering in I Peter is, however, much richer and more complex than this snippet would suggest. See Patricia M. McDonald, "The View of Suffering Held by the Author of I Peter," in Tambasco, *The Bible on Suffering*, pp. 165-87. I would call it the weak point of the epistle.

31 Louise Glück, "Matins (3)," in *The Wild Iris* (New York: Ecco Press, 1996), p. 12.

32 Louise Glück, "Matins (4)," ibid., p. 13.

33 Alistair McGrath, *Christian Theology* (Oxford: Blackwell Publishing, 2001), p. 292.

34 The idea that our suffering and struggle with evil is an essential part of our spiritual growth goes back to St. Ireneaus and persists today in the theology of John Hick (ibid., pp. 292-93).

35 D. Z. Phillips, *The Problem of Evil and the Problem of God* (Minneapolis, MN: Fortress Press, 2005), pp. 166, 179-80. Ireneaus, Hick, and Swinburne are leading proponents of this approach.

36 Simone Weil, Diogenes Allen, and D. Z. Phillips are proponents of this view. Allen insists that God's reality makes everything meaningful, even catastrophes: "[We] can trust that what we are doing and what is happening to us from the operations of the natural world and the social order make a contribution, even when we are not able to see that they do. All moments of dismay and dryness, as well as times of elation, make a contribution to that life which is being formed but which is not visible to us, especially when we are in states of distress" (*Christian Belief in a Postmodern World* [Louisville, KY: Westminster John Knox Press, 1989], p. 117). Later, in commenting on Adams's *Horrendous Evils*, Allen implicitly acknowledges that horrendous evils may serve no good purpose, but can only be redeemed by some counter-good that only God can offer. Simone Weil is the greatest exponent of the view that affliction ennobles, but it should be noted that Weil's life makes her subject to Soelle's accusation of masochism.

37 Aristotle and Thomas Aquinas were careful to distinguish between what we would call "causes" from what we would call "purposes."

38 Harold S. Kushner, *When Bad Things Happen to Good People* (New York: Schockten Books, 1981), pp. 133-34.

39 Ibid., 138.

40 John Macquarrie, *Principles of Christian Theology* (New York: Charles Scribner's Sons, 1977), p. 240.

41 "A world allowed to make itself through the evolutionary explorations of its potentiality is a better world than one produced by divine fiat. In such an evolving world, there must be some malfunctions and blind alleys. The same biochemical processes which allow some cells to mutate and produce new forms of life will allow other cells to mutate and become malignant. Entities will behave in accordance with their nature, as when tectonic plates slip and cause a devastating earthquake." John Polkinghorne, *Science and Theology: An Introduction* (Minneapolis: Fortress Press, 1998), p. 94.

42 Adams, *Horrendous Evils*, pp. 155-56.

43 Dominique Lapierre, *The City of Joy* (New York: Doubleday, 1985).

44 "Pippa Passes," in *Robert Browning*, by John Woolford and Robert Karlin (London: Longman, 1996), p. 116. Another view of the poem is that the little girl is voicing a heroic faith. From the 21st-century perspective, the poem looks ironic. Given the Victorian context, interpretation might go either way.

45 Hall, *God and Suffering*, p. 21.

46 Karl Marx, "A Contribution to the Critique of Hegel's Philosophy of the Right," (Paris, 1844), www.marxists.org/archive/marx/works/1843/critique-hpr/intro.htm.

47 See generally, J. Christiann Becker, *Suffering & Hope: The Biblical Vision and the Human Predicament* (Grand Rapids: Wm. B. Eerdmans Publishing Co., 1994)

48 Nicholas Wolterstorff, *Lament for a Son* (Grand Rapids, MI: Eerdmans, 1987), pp. 34-35.

49 MacLeish, *J. B.*, p. 110.

50 "The tradition of Jerusalem takes its stand on two basic affirmations concerning the human condition: the first is that suffering is real and is the existential lot of 'fallen' humanity.... The second is that suffering is not the last word about the human condition" (Hall, *God and Suffering*, p. 19).

51 Wright, *Evil and the Justice of God*, p. 40.

52 Jurgen Moltmann, *The Trinity and the Kingdom* (Minneapolis, MN: Fortress Press, 1980), p. 48.

53 James Weldon Johnson, "Lift Every Voice and Sing," in *Lift Every Voice and Sing*, ed. Horace Clarence Boyer (New York: Church Publishing, 1993), p. 1.

CHAPTER FIVE

GOD MAY NOT BE WHO YOU THINK GOD IS

I have administrative bones to pick with God, . . . I'll say God seems to have a laid-back management style I'm not crazy about. I'm pretty much anti-death. God looks by all accounts to be pro-death. I'm not seeing how we can get together on this issue, he and I . . .[1]
— David Foster Wallace

If we want to know how God responds to pain and sorrow, we must first sweep away false images of God. We must get clear on who God is not. There is a huge gaping flaw in the reasoning of "the problem of evil." The same flaw is there in all the explanations of suffering we have considered so far. They have assumed an image of God that is simplistic, inadequate and untrue to the ancient orthodox teachings of the Christian tradition. This chapter will debunk the false definition of God as the supreme omnipotent being who made the world and runs it to suit his fancy. That patriarchal picture of God is the key to "problem of evil."

GOD IS NOT THE SUPREME BEING

Many Christians never get past the children's Sunday school picture of God as "the man upstairs." Skeptics ask, "If Superman is out there, why doesn't he show up when we need him?" Even if we aren't so naively anthropomorphic as to think God is a man, we are apt to think he is a being along with the other beings in the universe, only bigger, stronger, smarter and older. Like the abominable snowman or intelligent aliens, such a being might or might not exist. However, if such a being does exist, he is not God. Orthodox, traditional theology teaches that God is not a being along with all the other beings, just bigger.[2] Our best contemporary theologians agree. As Kathryn Tanner says, "God is not a kind of thing among other kinds of things."[3] God is that out of which all being arises and into which all being sinks when it ceases to be. St. Paul said, "From him and through him and to him are all things," and "In him we live and move and have our being." God is the source, the destiny, and the meaning of reality. St. Augustine saw God as the ultimate object of all our longings.

Monotheism, if we stop to consider all that understanding of the divine nature means, is mind-boggling. When we say "God," we mean something vastly greater than polytheists would mean by "a god." We wrap so much up in the word "God." We know that all reality has a source. Exactly what it is, we can't say. But it begins somewhere, somehow, in something.[4] We also know that reality is in motion, in process, that history and evolution are moving forward toward something — and that something toward which it is moving may well be its purpose. The 20th-century Roman Catholic theologian, Karl Rahner, wrote of God as the source and the destiny of reality, "the whence and the whither" — "whence comest thou? whither goest thou?"

Likewise we hope there is some deep sense to reality, some order, some meaning. We believe that there is truth and that the truths we know, and the truths we do not yet know, may be ordered within an overarching, comprehensive structure of Truth, which we cannot know. We value things. Indeed, we hold that things actually have intrinsic value. And of all that is valuable, there must be that which is most valuable, ultimately valuable, something that finally matters. Just so, we delight in beauty, believing, or at least hoping, that there may be a greatest beauty beyond the reach even of our imagination.

Each of these things we have considered — source, destiny, meaning, sense, order, truth, value, beauty — could be its own object of devotion. Each could be regarded as a god. But monotheism rolls all of this and much more into the unified concept of God. Monotheism teaches that there is no final conflict between truth and beauty, that our source, our destiny, and our purpose are all one. All of this is in God. To put a point on it, God is very big — far too big to fit inside the universe. God does not fit inside anything. Everything must fit inside God. So God is not a being among other beings, a value among other values, a power among other powers.

A supreme being would be a being among other beings even if he is the biggest one. That is why such a being cannot be God.[5] The belief that God is both transcendent and immanent is central to Christian faith. "Transcendent" means utterly beyond reach — unsearchable because it is beyond the bounds of the universe, beyond the limits of reality itself. "Immanent" means present with us, permeating the creation, revealing itself in the smallest and subtlest movements of ordinary life. A supreme being is not truly transcendent because he[6] is inside the universe, a part of it. He is not truly immanent because he is not with us and in us. We do not "live and move and have our being" in him. He is just a giant dwelling somewhere in outer space. Unlike the supreme being, God is beyond the universe and yet within each grain of sand at the same time. God is our highest value, our moral order, our source, our destiny, and above all, God is the ultimate mystery beyond our reckoning.

If you have difficulty wrapping your mind around this way of thinking about God, you are on track. At most, only the tiniest fragment of God will fit inside your mind. Hence, the dictum of the father of Western theology, St. Augustine, "If you understand it, it is not God."[7] Christian doctrines don't wrap God up in a neat intellectual package for us to understand. Instead they point toward the mystery, giving us tentative images arising out of deep faith.

God is vastly more than a human, even a big one, but human images of God can still be helpful.[8] Such human language points toward God without denying that God is mystery. It does not literally limit God to the man upstairs. The point here is not that we must utterly discard thinking of God in human terms, but we must never limit God to human terms. For purposes of finding God in suffering, we start by giving up the notion that God is a being somewhere out there safe, while we are suffering here in the danger zone pleading with God to jump in and help. God is already here.

GOD IS NOT LITERALLY OMNIPOTENT

Atheist philosopher David Hume and his successors have defined God in terms of only two characteristics — goodness and power, with "power" being understood as total dominance or control. Hume understands dominating power to be the defining characteristic of God. Well, that is a seriously flawed understanding of God, and it makes "the problem of evil" intractable. Feminist theologians call that image of God "patriarchal." They are not necessarily rejecting the image of God as "father." "Patriarchal" here means God as dominator, as cosmic autocrat. The patriarchal God is God because he is omnipotent. God's literal omnipotence is the lynchpin of "the problem of evil" and the erroneous assumption in all the flawed attempts to answer the problem of evil.

Omnipotence is an oddly philosophical and peculiarly Greek notion about God — but it is one of the most widely accepted beliefs about God, even to the extent of understanding that God is God because God is omnipotent, that "God" means one who is omnipotent. If you and yours are free of this patriarchal God image, "the problem of evil" is probably not troublesome for you. But most people assume that divinity equals omnipotence, so the patriarchal picture of God persists dead center in "the problem of evil."

Bart Ehrman, in describing why he cannot believe in God, assumes that if God did exist, he would prove it by intervening in the world to impose his will. Even sophisticated theologians are not exempt from such ideas. Their "doctrine of God" chapters generally show a much richer sense of who God is. But, oddly enough, that is not the God who shows up in their "doctrine of evil" chapters. On this issue, even theologians who should know better lapse into patriarchal assumptions. So, we need to clear up a few things.

First, the concept of omnipotence is not to be found in scripture. We have expanded the biblical description of God as "almighty" into this notion of omnipotence. However, "almighty" in the Bible means "most powerful" — not literally omnipotent. The President of the United States is the "most powerful" political leader in the world, but he isn't omnipotent in global politics. Omnipotence is not a Hebrew concept. It comes from the Greek philosophical preference for absolute terms. Scripture does not support the doctrine of absolute literal omnipotence. In the Bible, things usually do not go God's way. If things always accorded with God's will in the Bible, the Divine would be in a better mood and would not have come off as so irritable in the prophets.

Moreover, absolute omnipotence does not make sense. I was once teaching a Great Books course to college freshmen who were greatly fond of their subjectivity. They insisted that each of us has one's own truth, one's own right, one's own wrong, and that no one should impose any kind of belief on another. At last the curriculum allowed me to ambush their subjectivity with Euclid. A student went to the board and proved by indubitable logic Euclid's theorem that parallel lines do not intersect. I questioned the class as to whether this might be true. "Yes," they said, "it is true." On cross-examination they held that it would be true even if a majority of us should vote that parallel lines henceforth would intersect. They held that no government could change this truth by decree, and that it had always and everywhere been true and would always be so, even in Singapore and Sweden. But when I asked them, "And what if God should decide that parallel lines intersect?" fully half the class insisted that then parallel lines would intersect despite the logical impossibility. Omnipotence leads people to say the strangest things!

Analytical philosophers point out that the notion of literal omnipotence is simply nonsense — "internally incoherent" is their term for it.[9] They demonstrate the senselessness of the word by asking questions such as, "Can God build a rock so big God cannot pick it up?"

Orthodox doctrines of the Church have never made such silly claims about God. The leading authorities in theology, the people who have defined the boundaries of the Church's faith, have always acknowledged that God's "omnipotence" does not mean God can do anything that is either logically inconsistent or foreign to God's nature. Medieval theologians such as Anselm, Thomas Aquinas and Duns Scotus, along with modern writers such as C. S. Lewis and D. Z. Phillips, all agree that "omnipotence" is subject to those two fundamental limitations.[10] The most influential Protestant theologian of the 20th century, Karl Barth rejected *"a priori* notions of omnipotence" — that is, the idea that whatever happens is the will of God. Barth maintained that the world is always threatened and often undone by the mysterious power of Nothingness (*das Nachtige*), which God did not create.[11]

Scripture, tradition and reason all oppose the view of God as literally omnipotent. Some theologians teach that God's power is limited by God's own nature.[12] For example, God cannot will evil.[13] Others say the nature of reality constrains God's power.[14] God cannot make the world flat and round at the same time. Others argue that God has deliberately limited God's own jurisdiction, withdrawn divine power, in order to let the cosmos be free and personal with a meaningful history instead of just playing out a script or dancing like a puppet.[15] These are variations on a single theme. God is not literally omnipotent.

Furthermore, equating God with absolute power is corrupting. It deifies power, not love. The celestial dominator, the big guy in the sky, the monarchical God is not the God of love represented by the Trinity. It is not the God revealed by Christ on the cross. The Christian God can also be manifest in weakness, defeat and suffering.[16]

The God on the cross renounces dominating or controlling power. Former Archbishop of Canterbury Rowan Williams places this decision to renounce power at the center of Christian theology. He writes, "The absence of God's manifest power is bound up with . . . a decision for powerlessness, against the domination of the world by manipulation . . . a decision to live with and within the potentially hurtful and destructive bounds of the world, a decision not to escape." He calls it a "decision for reality," coming to terms with things as they are — not passively or disengaged — but without trying to overcome the world with power.[17]

It is natural that we should stand in awe of the power of God. It is like the tornado effect. If the tornado doesn't kill us, we are at once thrilled and terrified by its force. Rudolf Otto, in his classic *The Idea of the Holy*, described the primal religious experience as an encounter with the *mysterium tremendum, mysterium fascinans* — an experience of simultaneous dread and fascination. God's power is awesome — but not absolute. The tornado is overwhelming, but there are many, many things a tornado cannot do. God can do more than a tornado because love is stronger than a big wind — but the difference between vast power and absolute dominance is huge.

We do not worship domination or worship because we are dominated. Once we have clarified that point, "the problem of evil" does not appear so daunting. The first premise simply does not hold water.[18] More importantly, once we get past the fixed assumption that divinity consists of dominating power, we can think anew about who God is. We can think far more creatively about how God responds to suffering and evil in the world.

GOD IS THE CREATOR — BUT MAYBE NOT LIKE YOU THINK.

At the core of our popular definition of God is that God is the one who designed, constructed, and rules the world subject to no limitations but his own unfettered will. To be fair, that view has deep roots in the Christian tradition, and it makes the problem of evil formidable. Since God created the universe, we hold God accountable for its defects. How we understand God's way of creating is even more important if we don't limit creation to something that happened a long time ago. Medieval and contemporary theologies teach a doctrine called *creatio continua*. It means God creates the universe anew in each moment. Modern physics brings this doctrine into sharp focus as it shows each moment arising out of something mysterious — not just happening automatically after the previous moment. When the moment is horrendous or just disappointing, we hold God all the more directly to blame.

When theologians describe the act of creation, they are actually speaking metaphorically about how God is involved in our world. If they were talking about the "how" of creation in a literal way, they would be trying to do science by guesswork. Creation models are not about science. They are ways of picturing how God is related to the world now. What is God doing? Is God connected to our lives? Can God be of any help? The way we describe God's creation of the world is a metaphor for how God is involved with us.

Our definition of "God" includes being the source of reality — but calling God the creator could mean different things. Just how does God "create" the universe? Let's look at four models of how creation might happen: (1.) Making; (2.) Emanation; (3.) Birthing; (4.) Withdrawing. These models make all the difference for how we understand the problem of evil and God's answer to it.

MAKING THE UNIVERSE: MAGIC OR ART

"Making" (or "constructing") means God creates the universe out of something or perhaps out of nothing at all. God is like an architect-contractor who designs everything and then brings it into existence by force of his own will. The picture of creation in Genesis looks like this sort of "making."

It is crucial here whether we think of the Creator as a magician pulling a rabbit out of a hat, making things appear out of thin air — or as a sculptor shaping formless matter into an orderly work of beauty. We do not start the argument with a clean slate. We have centuries of theology to consider — some good, some bad. St. Augustine's majestic explanation of why the world is as it is still haunts us. His doctrine of predestination, including the damnation of souls even before they were formed, all leading to a final cosmic good has huge moral holes — the ones Dostoevsky's Ivan Karamazov railed against. While Augustine wrote profound and beautiful theology, his explanation of the state of the world got off to a bad start with a regrettable doctrine called *creatio ex nihilo*, creation out of nothing.

The Bible does not say God created the world out of nothing. Rather in Genesis, God speaks light, life, and order into a dark, in-

GOD MAY NOT BE WHO YOU THINK GOD IS

animate chaos that God did not create.[19] Chaos — "formless and void" to quote Genesis directly — was just there from the beginning. The biblical model of making order out of chaos suggests where our problems come from. A tendency toward death and suffering remains embedded in the residual chaos of a world without form and void — Barth's nothingness. Physicists call it the law of entropy. Things tend to fall apart.

The Early Church developed the doctrine, *creatio ex nihilo*.[20] That version of "making" takes away the primordial source for disorder. *Creatio ex nihilo* makes the problem of evil more difficult because God fabricated even the raw materials of creation. In Genesis, God is a sculptor shaping chaos into orderly beauty, but Augustine's God was a magician making things appear out of less than thin air. This complication of the problem of evil is an accidental side effect of *creatio ex nihilo*. The point of that doctrine was to refute Gnosticism's

Photo: Zan Zig performing with rabbit and roses, magician poster, 1899 / From the Performing Arts Poster Collection at the Library of Congress.

claim that matter is evil, to defend the basic goodness of the material world — not to attribute suffering and evil to God.

Robert Farrar Capon went so far as to say that if God created the universe out of pre-existing raw material instead of out of nothing, the whole problem of evil would vanish. He wrote:

(There would be no problem of evil) if you believed that the world was made by God, not out of nothingness, but out of some primeval matter, Urstoff *or original glop which God didn't make and which he was simply stuck with. Then you could blame evil on the sleaziness of the raw materials he had to work with and get God off the hook by saying he is doing the best he can.*[21]

Capon dismisses this model of creation out of hand because he takes *creatio ex nihilo* to be a given. But creation from the primordial "glop" is the primary biblical metaphor of how the world came to be. The Hebrew scriptures regard evil as the force of residual chaos threatening to undo the cosmos (order) that sustains life and beauty. They took this understanding from their Sumerian and Canaanite neighbors and ancestors. Evil was the power of chaos. Chaos, represented in both pre-Jewish mythology and in the Hebrew scriptures as a sea monster or as the cosmic ocean itself, was the very raw material out of which God formed the cosmos.[22]

Describing creation in terms of whether God fabricated his own raw materials is too crude to take literally. The difference between making-from-chaos vs. making-out-of-nothing is really the question of omnipotence again.[23] *Creatio ex nihilo* suggests that God's hand was absolutely free in creation, that anything was possible. The implication is that God could have made any sort of universe he chose. The biblical doctrine of creation-out-of-chaos, on the other hand, suggests that there are certain limitations in the nature of things, that even though God could bring order out of chaos, chaos is still the primal state; so the tendency of things to fall apart is to be expected. The Second Law of Thermodynamics is mythically expressed in Genesis.

Yet, the belief that God creates the universe means God is involved in it, shaping and directing. In Genesis, God creates the light. God does not create the darkness. It is already there. God divides the light from the darkness. So God's hand is active in a positive, creative, life-giving way, smiling at the beauty of it all and saying "good." Attributing creation to God — not just "in the beginning" but always — is fundamental to our understanding of God's action. God creates. But chaos and destruction are not acts of creation.

EMANATING THE UNIVERSE: A LIGHT EXTENDING INTO THE DARKNESS

In the "Emanation" model, God is like the sun emanating rays; and the rays form creation.[24] Plotinus, the philosopher who most influenced Augustine, taught this view of creation and huge edifices of Christian theology would have been different if Augustine had gone along with him on this point instead of opting for *creatio ex nihilo*. Augustine turned away from Plotinus on the nature of creation, probably because emanation does not fit Genesis, but it is not completely at odds with all scriptural views of creation. Emanation has more Biblical support than *creatio ex nihilo* does. The prologue to John's Gospel suggests a creative emanation of light.

In the beginning was the Word, and the Word was with God and the Word was God. He was in the beginning with God and all things were made through him . . . In him was life and the light was the light of men. The light shines in the darkness and the darkness has not overcome it.[25]

In Hebrew scripture, God himself is above the earth, but the glory of God fills the earth. "Glory" is light shining forth from God. Emanation, that is to say God creating out of himself, has been a theme in the Christian tradition since our first great theologian, Origen of Alexandria, in the early 3rd century. The models of making and emanating are both part of the Christian tradition. Theologian John MacQuarrie cogently argued that they could coexist and correct each other, though neither model is adequate in itself.[26]

If we think of God creating by emanating into the empty darkness, God's presence is as light, as being, as the creative force — not destruction. But his emanation remains incomplete. So the forces of nothingness and death still have their dominion. Plotinus taught that Being overflowed, emanated into the emptiness of space. All the beings in the universe are expressions of that overflowing Being. The apparent evils or defects in reality are the limits of the emanation, the edges where Being thinned out and nothingness persisted. Much of the trouble in Western theology arises from Augustine's attempt to explain a universe that is fundamentally flawed, as Plotinus said it is, with a universe created by the fiat of a perfectly good God. If Augustine had allowed emanation to remain a part of his doctrine of creation, the problem of evil might never have become such a conundrum.

GIVING BIRTH TO THE UNIVERSE

There is yet a third way of describing the process of creation — the Birthing model.[27] One of the most strongly asserted images of God in Scripture is that of parent. To grasp this way of imagining creation, we need to get past thinking of God as male. The image of a God who gives birth is central to a feminist understanding of how suffering and generative power may co-exist in God.[28] The maleness of God is a limitation that will not do when we are trying to paint an adequate picture of the Creator. This model invites us to think of a Mother God giving birth to the cosmos. That image leads to a more coherent and more helpful way of picturing God's relationship with creation.

This model is considerably more helpful than "making." In a sense, parents create their children. But parents do not design and manufacture children to their own specifications. Children are born with a significant degree of free will, and are subject to a host of random influences and forces other than their parents. But they are also like their parents in important ways, and they are decidedly influenced and nurtured by their parents' love.

The metaphor of God giving birth to creation is well-attested in other ancient religions and is implicit in our calling God "Our Father."[29] Suggestions of creation as a giving birth are scattered through Scripture. For example, in Job 39, the Lord asks a series of rhetorical questions pointing toward himself. At verses 28-29, he says:

Has the rain a father,
  or who has begotten the drops of dew?
From whose womb did the ice come forth,
  and who has given birth to the hoarfrost of heaven?

In Acts Paul declares, "Indeed we are his offspring."[30]

The Birthing model of creation casts the problem of evil in a considerably different light. Even if a mother and father are good parents, their child may nonetheless suffer hardships. Their child may rebel and do things quite contrary to their parents' will. Yet loving parents remain faithful to the child. They help the suffering child as best they can. They encourage the errant child to reform. They invite the estranged child to come home. In his somewhat fictional "memoir"[31] of recovery from multiple chemical addictions, James Frey recounts the first time he telephoned his parents from a drug rehabilitation hospital.

Hi, Mom.
Hold on, James.
I hear her call my Father. My Father picks up the phone.
Hi, James.
Hi, Dad.
How are you?
All right.
How is it there?
It's fine.
What's happening so far?
I'm being detoxed and that sucks, and yesterday I moved down to the Unit and that's been fine.
Are you feeling like it's helping?
I don't know.
I hear my Mom take a deep breath.
Anything we can do?
I hear my Mom break down.
No.
I listen to her cry.
I gotta go.
You're gonna be okay, James. Just keep it up.
I listen to her cry.
I gotta go.
If you need anything, call us.
Good-bye.
We love you.
   I hang up the phone and I stare at the floor and I think about my Mother and my Father . . . and I wonder why they still love me and why I can't love them back and how two normal stable people could have created something like me. I stare at the floor and wonder.

When we think of God creating the universe, it is decidedly more helpful to imagine God giving birth to creation rather than manufacturing it. God is more powerful than earthly parents. God is eternal and earthly parents are not. The parent metaphor of God is inadequate. But it is more apt by far than the metaphor of the architect/contractor. The parent model shows a God who is involved without dominating.

MAKING ROOM FOR THE UNIVERSE

The final model of creation sounds less poetic, more metaphysical — so we must make a special effort to remember that this language is also a metaphor for a mystery. If God is by nature omnipresent, then how can God create something that isn't God? Where would God locate it? Even if we go back to the notion that God created the universe out of nothing, where was this nothing? Where was the emptiness that was not filled with God?

The answer of the Jewish Kabala and of some of our leading Christian theologians is that God withdraws into Godself, that creation begins by God pulling back to allow the space for creation. Theologians call this "self-limitation."[32] This way of imagining the act of creation goes back at least to the medieval Kabala, specifically Isaac Luria. He called God's creative act *zimsum*, meaning "concentration," "contraction," or withdrawal into the self.[33] One might think of God withdrawing Being in order to allow the emptiness or nothingness where creation is formed, and which remains at the core of everything so that things that exist are ever on the verge of falling out of existence. Or we might think of God withdrawing order to allow the chaos out of which reality is formed, so that order is always on the verge of falling apart — a situation physicists express as the law of entropy.

This way of imagining creation means God is to some degree absent and not in control of our world. God's absence allows evil room to operate. But if God were fully present, the world could not exist. There would be no room for it. If God's will decided everything, then there would be no other will in the universe and hence no other person — only God. Simone Weil said:

The act of creation is not an act of power. It is an act of abdication. Through this act a kingdom was established other than the kingdom of God. The reality of this world is constituted by the mechanism of matter and the autonomy of rational creatures. It is a kingdom from which God has withdrawn.[34]

God's ability to alleviate suffering is limited primarily because of the way creation happens. God creates by allowing something to exist that absolutely is not God. If the universe were entirely under God's control, it would just be an extension of God, not an independent reality. God allows the universe to exist in freedom from divine control.[35] Allowing such freedom is like giving the car keys to one's teenager. It's risky. God is not in direct control. That is why C. S. Lewis can say that the world is "in enemy hands" and Paul can say the world is subject to "the powers and the principalities of this present age." God is not pulling the strings like a puppet master, making things happen like a magician.

God's "self-limitation" cannot be absolute. If God completely withdrew being, there would be only nothingness. If God withdrew all order, there would be only chaos. So obviously God is somewhat present generating being and order. Instead of imagining God as completely abandoning the field, it may be more apt to think of God thinning out the divine presence. We might think of this as the opposite of Plotinus' emanation. Instead of God's light emanating out in creation, it withdraws to make room for the necessary darkness. Either way, the divine nature thins out at the edges. If we allow for that nuance of God somewhat present, but not fully present, it makes sense to acknowledge that God has to allow the universe to function outside his control because that is the only way it could be created at all.[36]

This model of creation helps us understand an important point about God's will that most theologians accept — the distinction between *active will* and *permissive will*. God may actively make some things happen, like healing and reconciliation. God's nature makes it impossible for God to actively "*will* evil" (physical or moral) even for a passing time or to serve an ulterior greater good.[37] But God may *permit* other things to happen, like illness and conflict. God's permitting something does not mean God likes it. It means God allows the existence of that which is not under divine control. God does not afflict us as part of some plot in which the end justifies the means.

God does not specifically will evil either actively or permissively. God permits the creation to be outside divine control. That in itself is not evil but good. The evil that happens within that freedom is not God's will. As Hart puts it, ""(W)hat God permits, rather than violate the autonomy of the created world, may be *in itself* contrary to what he wills."[38] But remember that God's withdrawal is not complete. Divine presence is thinned out, not utterly absent. God's refusal to control a situation does not mean God is not present, participating, and eager to influence for the good.

The only picture of creation that makes the problem of evil intractable is the idea that God designs and manufactures reality perfectly to suit his own will. Even the making model doesn't portray God as exercising such absolute dominion if we remember the biblical view that God starts with the raw material of chaos and that chaos remains residually chaotic and disruptive of the divine order. Emanation shows God risking God's own being to create the world that is beyond divine control. Birthing shows God engendering creation out of love, like a parent, not constructing it to fit specifications. The idea that God has to withdraw, or at least thin out, to allow space for the world means our very existence depends on God being somewhat removed, somewhat hands off.

These models of creation may be at least as helpful as the attempted explanations of evil in helping us understand why God permits suffering. But more importantly, they are our first hint of how God is connected to this joy-grief of life we are given. They show us a God actively participating in the creation, participating lovingly and creatively, shining into the darkness. After all, we are not really in the business of explaining and justifying suffering. We are not in the business of defending evil and affliction. Our project is showing how God helps and how we can find hope. Hope is our stock and trade.

CONCLUSION

When we studied the answers to the problem of evil, they weren't satisfactory, because the God they assumed was not a satisfactory God. They assumed a supreme being standing outside the universe choosing to intervene or not. They assumed a literally omnipotent God who could waive a magic wand and make everything alright if he only chose to do so. They assumed a God who designs and manufactures each moment out of his unfettered will. The God those answers assume is not a God who evokes our love and is not a God who seems inclined to save us from our plight. Now we have repudiated that unhelpful way of imagining who God is. Next we will invite the possibility of a different way of understanding God, a way that could make all the difference to how we face our own hardships and how we respond to those of others.

REFLECTION QUESTIONS

1. Have you heard God described in ways that assume God is a being or the Supreme Being? What are the images or the assumptions in that idea about who God is and what God can do?

2. Have you heard God described in ways that do not make God a being or the Supreme Being? What are the images and what are the assumptions in that idea about what God can and cannot do?

3. Do you assume God has to be omnipotent to be God? If something were omnipotent and evil, would it be God? If something were perfectly good, true, and beautiful, but not omnipotent, what would it be?

4. Look back at the different ways of describing how God creates the universe. Which of them appeals to you? Which of them makes most sense? What difference does each model of creation make for our understanding of who God is and how God is related to the world?

5. If God is conceived as an architect/contractor, just how good an architect contractor is he?

6. If God were conceived as a parent, what kind of parent would you say God is?

7. How do you experience God as present in the world?

8. How do you experience God as absent from the world?

NOTES

1   David Foster Wallace, *Infinite Jest* (New York: Back Bay Books, 1996), p. 40.

2   David Bentley Hart, *The Beauty of the Infinite* (Grand Rapids: Wm. B. Eerdmans Publishing Co., 2003), p. 164.

³ Katherine Tanner, *Jesus, Humanity, and Trinity*. (Minneapolis: Fortress Press. 2001) p. 4. Kyoto philosopher Keiji Nishitani says, both Being and Nothingness float in an Absolute foundation, which Christians call "God." In the 13th century, Thomas Aquinas called God "Being." In the 20th century, Paul Tillich called God "the ground of Being," the "depth of existence." They use these terms to say that God is not a being alongside other beings. God is rather the foundation of reality itself.

⁴ We may thing of this source temporally as in the originator or creator of the universe. Or we may think of it *ontologically* as the foundation, which now holds things in being.

⁵ Orthodox theologian David Bentley Hart takes to task modern theologies that "trade in mythology, . . . preach a finite God, one who is no doubt a 'supreme being,' but not the source of all being." David Bentley Hart, *The Doors of the Sea: Where Was God in the Tsunami?* (Grand Rapids: Wm. B. Eerdmans Publishing Co., 2005), p. 78.

⁶ I may sometimes use the masculine pronoun as it is used, albeit regrettably, as inclusive of the female. I do not mean to suggest that God is male, and will minimize the use of the masculine pronoun to refer to God. However, when I speak of this Supreme Being idea of God, I use the masculine pronoun advisedly because Supreme Being theology invariably does regard God as male. That is part of what is wrong with it.

⁷ Augustine, *Sermons* 52, Ch. 1, no. 16.

⁸ Robert Farrar Capon argues that we need more anthropomorphic talk about God, not less. Robert Farrar Capon, *Hunting The Divine Fox: Images and Mystery in Christian Faith* (New York: Seabury Press, 19974) pp. 7-11. Jurgen Moltmann says the incarnation reveals that there is a quality in God that we can rightly call "humanity." Jurgen Moltmann, *The Trinity and the Kingdom* (Minneapolis: Fortress Press, 1993), p. 118.

⁹ D. Z. Phillips, *The Problem of Evil and the Problem of God*, pp. 3-21.

¹⁰ Alister McGrath, *Christian Theology*, (Oxford: Blackwell Publishing, 2001) pp. 281-282. Phillips demonstrates that "There are countless activities it does not make sense to attribute to God" because what God can do depends on who or what you believe God is. D. Z. Phillips, *The Problem of Evil and the Problem of God*, pp. 3-22.

11 Alister McGrath, *Christian Theology*, p. 294.

12 Alister McGrath, *Christian Theology*, p. 295. D. Z. Philips develops this point at some length in *The Problem of God and the Problem of Evil*.

13 David Bentley Hart, *The Doors of the Sea*, p. 70.

14 Philosophers call the restraints imposed by logic "eternal compossibilities." The world can be round or flat, but not both.

15 Alister McGrath, *Christian Theology*, pp. 281-284. We will look more closely at self-limitation in the next chapter in the context of creation. This is the most helpful understanding of the limits of divine power for purposes of explaining suffering. See also D. Z. Phillips, *The Problem of Evil and the Problem of God*, p. 181.

16 Shirley Guthrie, *Christian Theology*, at p. 112.

17 Rowan Williams, *On Christian Theology*. (Oxford: Blackwell Press, 2000), p. 122. J. R. R. Tolkien's *Lord of the Rings* trilogy is about this kind of religion. In *Lord of the Rings*, there are good guys and bad guys. The bad guys are threatening the good guys — but the good guys have a magical ring that gives them vast power. The problem is that using the power will turn them into bad guys. The power of the ring corrupts. So their goal is to destroy the ring, and their constant moral challenge is to refrain from using it. *Lord of the Rings* was written during World War II, and it has the marks of World War II all over it. So, as we might expect, it reflects the theology of one of the greatest theologians from that time, Reinhold Niebuhr. Notwithstanding Tolkien's Catholicism and Niebuhr's Protestantism, they shared some theological perspectives evoked by that time of crisis. Niebuhr said our greatest danger lay not in the evil in the world but in the power used to restrain that evil. Our own power was more dangerous than Hitler.

18 Alvin Plantinga observes that the argument against faith actually depends on additional premises about what an omnipotent God can do and on what a good God *will* do. Plantinga's argument is too intricate to recount here. But suffice it to say that:
   1. Omnipotence does not entail being able to do logically inconsistent things (draw a square circle, etc.). There at least may be good things that, as a matter of logic, cannot be preserved without also preserving

a corresponding evil (parable of the wheat and the tares situation). The freedom to choose between good and evil is such a good thing. That freedom depends on evil being an available option.

2. Goodness does not require God to eradicate every evil, especially if such an evil cannot be eradicated without also destroying something good. Alvin C. Plantinga, *God, Freedom, and Evil* (Grand Rapids: Wm. B. Eerdmans Publishing Co., 1974), pp. 10, 12-34; Peterson, pp. 17-18.

[19] Alister McGrath calls this model "ordering" and notes that it is the predominant Old Testament view, and that the earliest Christian theologians assumed God created the universe out of pre-existent matter. Alister McGrath, *Christian Theology*, pp. 296-297.

[20] McGrath, *Christian Theology*, pp. 296-298.

[21] Robert Farrar Capon, *The Third Peacock* (Garden City: Doubleday, 1971), p. 15.

[22] Joseph Kelly, *The Problem of Evil in the Western Tradition* (Collegeville: The Liturgical Press, 2002), pp. 8-11.

[23] Karl Barth understood God's relationship to creation in terms of the biblical model of bringing a cosmos out of chaos and preserving the cosmos from the ever-present potential of chaos. David Bentley Hart vigorously repudiates Barth's argument, calling it "the most malign of mythic narratives" because it suggests an eternal dualism: God vs. Chaos. David Bentley Hart, *The Beauty of the Infinite*, pp. 257-259. Hart, however, is ready to avoid dualism of God vs. Evil by saying evil or sin is not a "thing." Relying on the doctrine of *privatio boni*, he insists sin has no being. It is not created. We might say the same of chaos. In any event, the point of this biblical image of creation, for our purposes, is not to posit an eternal dualism, but merely to say that the tendency toward chaos is a given in reality, not something God "created" any more than God could be said to have created darkness, death or sin.

[24] John Macquarrie, *Principles of Christian Theology*, p. 218.

[25] John 1: 1-5.

[26] John Macquarrie, *Principles of Christian Theology*, pp. 217-222.

27 The Creeds reserve the image of begetting for the second person of the Trinity and not for the rest of creation. That, however, is to emphasize that the Son is God just as the Father is God; whereas, the creation is not God. In this respect the Birthing model could be misleading. But that does not preclude us from using it in this context to supplement the Making and Emanating views of Creation. The Birthing model is not meant to suggest that the creation is God. If this metaphor fails to convey the difference between Creator and creation, then let that point be clarified. God is God and the creation is not. This metaphor of creation is intended to mean the creation is generated and sustained by Divine Love, that it is free, and its proper stance toward God is that of a child toward a parent.

28 Patricia Fox, *God as Communion*. (Collegeville: The Liturgical Press, 2001), p. 153.

29 Jesus taught his disciples to use this term long before Pauline theology said we become in a fuller sense the sons of God through our identification with Jesus. So Jesus taught that we are already, even in a pre-Christian state, God's children in some sense. We are children in the sense that he gives us our being, but with freedom.

30 Acts 17: 28.

31 James Frey, *A Million Little Pieces* (New York: Random House, 2003) pp. 43-44. Frey's book is partly memoir, partly fiction. Whether this conversation actually happened between Frey and his parents or not is beside the point for us. It is a conversation that has happened between many parents and many addicted sons and daughters.

32 Kenotic theology, the idea of God limiting himself, began in the 19th century as a way of understanding the Incarnation. Gottfried Thomasius, F. H. R. von Frank, W. F. Gess, Charles Gore, and P. T. Forsyth then advanced it. Alister McGrath, pp. 283-284. As a model of creation it has found support today from Rowan Williams, Jurgen Moltmann, and (to some extent) John Macquarrie.

33 Moltmann, *The Trinity and the Kingdom*, pp. 108-111.

34 Simone Weil, "Are We Struggling For Justice?" trans. Marina Barabas, *Philosophical Investigations*, Vol 10, No 1 (January 1987), p. 3 quoted in D. Z. Phillips, *The Problem of Evil and the Problem of God*, p. 181. Phillips endorses Weil's view that creation is not an act of power.

35 This is a kenotic theology idea. It does not necessarily posit that God has limits within God's own nature. It does say that God has voluntarily surrendered his intrinsic power in order to allow the existence of a free and personal creation which is not a mere extension or alter ego of the Creator.

36 There are two schools of thought relating to limits on the power of God. Some process theologians and linguistic analytical theologians see these limitations as inherent in God. They see God as being, from the beginning, and as result of God's very nature, unable to do some things. Others, sometimes called kenotic theologians, including Simone Weil, see God as having created the world though self-limitation. They say God in God's nature is essentially omnipotent, but God has relinquished some of the divine power in order to allow the universe to exist. For our purposes, it may not matter much which way things came to this state. Either way, there are real limits, on what God can do for us.

37 David Bentley Hart, *The Doors of the Sea*, p. 70.

38 David Bentley Hart, *The Doors of the Sea*, p. 82. I do not think Adams would disagree. Though she would probably say that God's reasons for allowing the creation such autonomy are mysterious.

CHAPTER 6

Then what do we say about God?

There is no word that is more difficult to use appropriately than 'God'."
— Nicholas Lash, *The Beginning and End of Religion*

*If God is a dog drowsing
contemplating
the quintessential dogginess
of the universe, of the whole
canine race, why are we
uneasy?
No dog I know
would hurl thunderbolts
or plant plague germs
or shower us with darts
of pox or gonococci.
No. He lies on his back
awaiting the cosmic belly rub,
he wags his tail signifying
universal love; he frolics and cavorts . . .
But God is all too human . . .*
— Erica Jong, "If God Is a Dog" from *At the Edge of the Body*

'God" is a rich word, the richest word. Liberating it from the patriarchal image, the big guy in the sky dominating everything, breaks open the way to see more of who God is. We could write shelves full of books about God. But for purposes of this book, we will look at just a few characteristics of God that mean God can sustain and empower us in the face of tragedy — without being a dominator.

God is our moral azimuth — the North Star that orients all our values — and our values orient our actions, indeed our whole life. What makes God "God" in our eyes defines what we believe life is about. If God is God by virtue of absolute power, we worship power. If God is God by virtue of knowing everything, we worship knowledge. If God is God by virtue of being the judge of all, we worship judgment.

We become like the God we believe in. Our image of God determines what we esteem, what we do, and ultimately who we become.[1] A God who is waiting on the edge of his seat to exact wrathful judgment on a fallen world will have worshipers who judge New York or Baghdad to be evil and bomb the wicked city to oblivion. Because God is the infinite mystery, we cannot prove our beliefs about God with ordinary evidence. But we can discern good religion from bad religion by the effect of the religion on the characters of its adherents. "By their fruits shall you know them." There are a lot of bad ideas about God claiming to be Christian views, or worse the Christian view. When we come up against disaster, in times of crisis, we are especially apt to latch onto bad images of God, and those bad images do not serve us well over time. As Archbishop William Temple said, "If you have a false idea of God, the more religious you are the worse it is for you — it were better for you to be an atheist".[2]

In this chapter, we will rethink the meaning of the word "God." We will ask seriously, "What are the defining characteristics of God? What makes God God?" As we examine any doctrine of God, we can test it by asking: is this picture of God truly our highest value? Is this image of God genuinely beautiful? Is this God the kind of person we want to become? Our goal in this book is to speak of God in ways that console, strengthen, empower, and liberate — to engage in "emancipatory God-talk."[3] So let's examine a few of the basic things the Christian tradition has said about God, things which make all the difference for how God responds to suffering.

GOD IS LOVE

St. John teaches us that God's very essence is love.[4] We experience God's love in blessings, as the General Thanksgiving in *The Book of Common Prayer*[5] puts it, "our creation, preservation and all the blessings of this life, . . . the means of grace and the hope of glory."[6] Love, not power, is the defining essence of God, the very godness of God. God is God not by virtue of omnipotence, but by virtue of omni-love, omni-delight, omni-compassion. This is a claim about the meaning and value of existence that runs directly counter to power-narrative Christianity. Canadian theologian Douglas John Hall, speaking particularly of his own Lutheran tradition, says:

Because for Luther human existence is a frail and uncertain business, divinity for him is not first of all sovereign omnipotence (as it was for Calvin) but astonishing compassion.[7]

Even before there was a world for God to love, God was already loving. There was a beginning of the universe and the universe will come to an end. But there is no beginning and no end to the divine love out of which the universe is born and into which it will finally merge.

God's love is irreconcilably inconsistent with literal omnipotence because divine love is not just affection for what pleases God. Princeton theologian Diogenes Allen aptly expresses the way God loves when he describes how we are called to love. Allen says we are to love everything in the realm of reality *that is independent of us*. In other words, we love it even if we can't control it, and therefore it is not precisely as we would like it to be. Allen writes,

(W)e must love that which is absolutely independent of us. We do recognize differences between good and evil, between suffering and happiness. But . . . we are to love them nonetheless; that is, we are not to allow our tastes, desires, preferences, notions of utility, or even our moral judgments to prevent our loving them . . . (T)o remove the self is to prevent the operation of our tastes, desires, ideas of utility and the rest from (blinding us to) things as they are — whether useless or useful, good or bad, painful or pleasant, they are to be loved, as a whole and in each detail, because they are there.[8]

As long as we are in control, we do not really love things as they are. We love rather the reflection of our own wills, the satisfaction of getting our own way. Loving only what suits our tastes is like gazing fondly into a mirror. To really love is to delight in and cherish things that are not as we would have them be. Human love is so readily ensnared in and twisted by our compulsion to judge! So To speak of loving that which does not please us, that which is not as we would have it be, we have to imagine love greater than we can experience. At best we know a hint of it on rare occasions.

Divine love appreciates the sheer reality of something, the suchness of it, its very independence from control. God creates that which is not God, so that God can love an other, love those who are truly different — even that which is ungodly. God relinquishes control so that God can flow out of Godself in love for that which is not God, that which is not like God, that which is not as God would choose for it to be. God loves a world that is sometimes utterly unlovable in our eyes.

Divine love shocks our sensibilities. When Jesus revealed divine love, people were appalled. Does this mean God loves sin and evil? It helps here to remember Augustine: Evil is not a thing to be loved or hated; sin is love disordered. God loves the love that motivates the sinner, even though the sinner's love is disordered. God's love recognizes the distinction between good and evil. God loves into them both, but loves differently. The good is loved with celebration and delight. The evil is loved *into* (note the all important preposition) with grief and reconciling invitation. But God always values the suchness, the is-ness, the being of everyone and everything.

Students routinely ask me, "What about Adolph Hitler? Does God love Hitler? Must we love Hitler?" Simone Weil was the theologian most radically committed to belief in God's all-inclusive unconditional love. Weil died in 1943 as an active participant in the Free French resistance, but she would insist on loving Hitler. Love in the face of evil manifests as resistance, not acquiescence or condonation.

Once we realize that literal omnipotence and love are mutually exclusive, we have to make a choice. Will we define God as Perfect Love or Total Dominance? Scripture, logic, and much of the Christian tradition are on the side of love. But ultimately we have to search our own hearts. The word "God" represents our most deeply held value. "God" means what we hold to be the highest good, the truest truth, the loveliest beauty. So, what do we regard as the most valuable, the most important thing — love or dominance?

A God of love instead of power may not be what we want in the face of life's troubles. Some of us are reluctant to accept that God's power is limited because those limitations might undermine our trust that God can deliver us. That objection, however, rests on the assumption that our problems can be solved by power. Much human suffering cannot be redeemed by powerful interventions, understanding "power" to mean dominance and control, but it can be redeemed by divine love. As Douglas John Hall says,

> Who through power tactics, can eliminate the self-destroying habits of a son or daughter fallen prey to hard drugs? What nation through power alone can ensure world peace? . . . There is no sword that can cut away sin without killing the sinner . . . (T)here are situations where power is of no avail. They are most of the situations in which we human beings find ourselves! . . . They are most of the situations God finds God's Self in too.[9]

There are better ways than dominating power — not quick fixes, but ways that genuinely redeem us and make us whole. Love is power like the electricity that lights a lamp, or fire that warms us on a cold night. Love heals and redeems. That is God's kind of power. To change our understanding of God requires us to rethink *how* we hope to be saved from affliction. To change our understanding of God requires us to rethink our assumption that problems can be solved by Rambo-style interventions.

GOD IS BEAUTIFUL

How late I came to love thee, O Beauty, so ancient and so fresh.
  — St. Augustine of Hippo

Beauty is the chief attribute of God according to 18th-century American Calvinist, Jonathan Edwards. David Bentley Hart cites the Church Fathers in support of Edwards' view:

> God is beauty and also beautiful, whose radiance shines upon and is reflected in his creatures . . . the splendor that gathers all things . . . into itself. (De divinis nominibus 4.7).[10]

Scripture attests to the beauty, the splendor and the glory of God.[11] St. Gregory of Nyssa retold the story of Moses as a quest for the beatific vision, for the ever-expanding beauty of God.

> Moses: though he is filled to overflowing, says Gregory, he always thirsts for more of God's beauty . . . ; and such is the action of every soul that loves beauty: drawn on forever by a desire enkindled always anew by the

beauty that lies beyond the beauty already possessed, receiving the visible as an image of God's transcendent loveliness . . .[12]

Consider the implications for our relationship with God, and for our sense of what life is about, if we thought of God primarily in terms of beauty to be enjoyed rather than dominating power to be feared. This ancient understanding of God has been understated in recent centuries. But today we are in the midst of a reawakening of theological aesthetics, and are rediscovering the relationship between art and religion.[13]

What does God's beauty have to do with God's response to suffering? Perhaps everything. Philosopher Marilyn McCord Adams says that God's beauty redeems even "horrendous evils," the kinds of suffering which make life seem no longer worth living. Her argument rests on the following points:

1. God is so unimaginably greater than creation that God is of a totally different order from our earthly experience or us.

2. God's goodness includes God's beauty, which is immeasurably greater than "created goods or ills."

3. "Contemplation of Divine Beauty" engulfs the harm we have suffered, even "horrendous evils."[14]

God redeems by the power of Divine Beauty to attract, console, and heal rather than the power of domination.[15] Desire is the tug of the infinitely beautiful vortex that is God. Delight, the culmination of desire, is our foretaste of ultimate joy. Even horrors grow dim in the light of resplendent glory. St. Paul said, "I consider that the sufferings of this present time are not worth comparing to the glory that is to be revealed to us."[16]

This hope for healing in the "kindly light" of God's glory does not mean some greater good of cosmic order justifies the sacrifice of individual victims. In order to fit the goodness of God, the restoration must be sufficient to make each and every victim of evil whole, to give them such a good thing that it makes their life worthwhile despite the horrors they have endured. Such horrors are so great that they can be defeated only by the incomparable goodness of God.[17]

The redemption of each individual is essential to the morality of

THEN WHAT DO WE SAY ABOUT GOD?

God. Ivan Karamazov lamented over the suffering of a little girl left to freeze in an outhouse on a Russian winter night. To his credit, he would not have his own eternal bliss purchased by such an atrocity. But finally, Ivan has missed the point. The little girl's suffering does not purchase his eternal bliss. Her eternal bliss redeems her from the atrocity she suffered — an atrocity that was not part of God's plan but was always contrary to God's will. David Bentley Hart, who takes Ivan's argument quite seriously and respects Ivan's protest as essentially Christian, says:

> ... (O)ne might even suspect Ivan of a willingness to freeze (the little girl) forever in the darkness of her torments — as a perpetual symbol of his revolt against heaven — rather than release her into a happiness he thinks unjust.[18]

Heaven, the beatific vision, eternal bliss — our destiny in union with God — is not a cosmic good purchased by the blood and tears of individuals. Rather it is the redemption of each individual from wrongs that were just that — wrongs — torments that should never have had to be endured. It is finally arriving at the joy upon which "the strange beauty of the world" depends.

Most of us have not yet experienced the beatific vision. So, we might draw a metaphor from a picture taken by the Hubble telescope. This instrument is placed so far out from earth that its view is not impaired by atmosphere, dust or any obstacles (as our view will be unimpaired when the created order falls away). Through the Hubble telescope, we see a starry swirling vortex of colorful light that is so beautiful astronomers have dubbed it "the eye of God." It is breath-takingly splendid. God's beauty must immeasurably exceed even this marvelous spectacle. Imagine that God is so awe-inspiring, so evocative of our love, that we will be as the song says "lost in wonder, love and praise." It is immersion in that sea of adoration that heals and redeems the wounds we have suffered.

GOD IS EVERYWHERE

Whither shall I go from thy presence?
Whither shall I flee from thy presence O God?
If I ascend up into heaven, thou art there.
If I make my bed in hell, behold thou art there.
If I take the wings of the morning,
  and dwell in the uttermost parts of the sea;
  even there thy hand shall lead me
  and thy right hand shall hold me.
    — Psalm 139

Since God is the foundation of reality, there can be no reality where God is not. Theologians call this attribute "omnipresence." Since God is the ground of Being, nothing exists except by standing on God. If God is loving, beautiful, and just, the divine presence is a consolation in the face of affliction. We know that wherever we are, in whatever circumstances, God is our foundation and our strength. God is omnipresent not only geographically, but also situationally. God is present when we are in despair, not just when we are elated. God is present when we are afraid and angry. God's presence reaches all situations.

Elie Wiesel relates this story from at Auschwitz:

The SS hung two Jewish men and a boy before the assembled inhabitants of the camp. The men died quickly but the struggle of the boy lasted half an hour. "Where is God? Where is he?" a man behind me asked. As the boy, after a long time, was still in agony on the rope, I heard the man cry again," Where is God now?" And I heard a voice within me answer, "Here he is — hanging here on the gallows."¹⁹

The answer is equivocal. It could mean that this stark case of "the problem of evil" makes belief in God impossible. Or it could mean that even in this most awful moment God is present, suffering the worst that evil inflicts. If God is present when a child is being hanged, what is God doing? How is God present in affliction? God is present with all the divine attributes even in the face of atrocities. God's love weeps at suffering. God's beauty is present as a hope that the rainbow will come after the storm. God's justice cries out against oppression and demands the restoration of moral relationship. God is present at the gallows as compassion and hope and protest.

GOD IS NEAR AND FAR

Behold the word is very near to you.
It is in your mouth and in your heart.
   — Moses

The kingdom of God is within you.
   — Jesus

To grasp the profundity of all these characteristics of God, it helps to remember that God is with us right up close, "nearer to you than you are to yourself" as Meister Eckhart said. Yet God is vastly beyond the reach or our imagination. In short, God is very big. Theologian Shirley Guthrie used the opening of the Lord's Prayer. "Our Father in heaven," to show how we understand God as both right here with us (theologians say "immanent"; Scripture says "near"[20]) and yet absolutely out of reach, so far beyond our brand of reality we can't even begin to imagine it (theologians say "transcendent"; Scripture says "far."[21]). "Our Father" is a name that says God is near to us, intimately related to us. "In Heaven" reminds us that God is infinitely far above us.[22]

When we say God is distant or far away, we don't mean God is geographically a long way off. God's distance is a metaphor with several meanings. John Hick says God's distance means God is utterly incomprehensible to us, absolutely mysterious.[23] In Scripture we hear of the imageless One whom people call YHWH, but who has never truly revealed his name, and who cannot be contained in a Temple or even in the whole world. [24]

To get a sense of God's transcendence, it helps to remember some of God's other essential characteristics and then do an exercise with them to stretch our imaginations. As we have seen, theologians from Augustine to Jonathan Edwards to Hans Urs Von Balthasar have understood God as the greatest Beauty. Think of the most beautiful thing you have ever encountered, perhaps a work of art or music, perhaps something in nature, whatever has been most beautiful to you. Now up the scale by imagining something more beautiful than that. Imagine the greatest beauty you possibly can. Now believe that there is a beauty even greater, a beauty beyond the reach of your imagination.

Now think of goodness not as moral purity, but as worth or value. Think of what is most valuable to you. Then imagine something more valuable. Imagine the greatest value there could possibly be. Then believe there is something more valuable. Now think of what is the most foundational truth, a truth on which all other truths depend. It may be something like "There is something rather than nothing." Then stretch your imagination toward a deeper truth, such as "There is a cause, reason, and purpose that there is something rather than nothing. (Aquinas called it "Being." Tillich called it the "Ground of Being.") Now believe that some unimaginable truth lies behind even that. When your soul "has stretch(ed) when reaching out of sight for the ends of being and ideal grace," you are looking toward the transcendence of God.

When we speak of God's transcendence, we mean a kind of distance. There is much of God we cannot touch or begin to imagine. On the other hand, God sometimes seems near to us. God wants us to know him. God longs for an intimate relationship with us. Scripture says God's Word, Spirit, Wisdom and Glory, are active and manifest in our midst. This is the immanent God. When people speak of experiencing God in their hearts, or when we say God acts or happens in moments of love, mercy, justice or beauty, or when scientists like Paul Davies or Steven Hawking speak of their research as exploring "the mind of God," they are saying God is immanent, with us, intimate, knowable.[25]

Both aspects of God will have to be part of our understanding of suffering. A God who is only transcendent cannot identify with us or truly care about our suffering. That God is too far above us — too alienated from the mess and muddle of our frail lives. A God who is only immanent will be unable to lift us up from our broken world because such a God is stuck down here in the same world we are. A God who is only immanent cannot help us. A God who is only transcendent will not help us. But a God who is paradoxically both immanent and transcendent, now there is a God who might offer hope — even if such a paradoxical God is harder to understand.

GOD IS PERSONAL

All the answers lie in faith; and when you lose your faith you have no choice but to substitute for it a philosophy that deliberately and coldly offers no answers at all.
    — Simon Mawer, The Gospel of Judas[26]

In Simon Mawer's novel, *The Gospel of Judas*, Fr. Leo Newman is a scholar on his way to losing his faith. In his prayer, we see his faith slipping away.

He prayed to a God who veered between the patriarchal mythic figure and an abstract concept as vast as the galaxy, as vast as the space between the galaxies, as vast and nebulous and meaningless as the space that contained all the galaxies and all the spaces.[27]

    The vastness of God, who inhabits the entire universe and is infinitely beyond it, tempts us to think God is abstract, like a law of nature. Yet Christians have experienced God as deeply personal. God is even vaster than our quotation from *The Gospel of Judas* says. But that does not make God "abstract," "nebulous and meaningless." Wrong as it is, the "patriarchal mythic figure" is closer to a true picture of God than an "abstract concept" would be. When we think of something vast, we may leap to the conclusion it is impersonal. But the mind-boggling thing about God is the combination that God is both vast and personal — the ground of reality that holds "all the galaxies and their spaces" is personal.

    When we say God is "personal" we mean that God feels, wills, thinks, believes, remembers. We also mean God is relational, that God lives in relationship, longs for relationship. God must be personal in order to be God, because being personal is a positive attribute. If God were not personal, God would be less than we are.

A God who has no thoughts or feelings would be a lower being than a human being who is capable of thinking and feeling.

Our own personhood emerged from God's creation. The impersonal cannot generate personhood. We experience God as personal. God touches us, speaks to us, cares for us. The God we meet in prayer and contemplation is warm and compassionate.[28] But the personhood of God is different from human personhood, because God is not limited by an ego-center. God isn't constrained by his own private agendas, by seeing others in terms of how they affect his interests, by needing his existence validated. When we think of God as "a person" lording it over creation, God isn't very attractive. But God is not limited as human persons are. Rather God has all the strengths and capacities that go with being personal and relating to others personally — without the limitations.

If God is personal and relates to us interpersonally, we may ask whether we can influence God. Is God subject to being changed by us? God's will about specific things can be changed. God is genuinely responsive. If God could not change at all, God would not be responsive and would not be fully personal. But God's essential character is fixed. We cannot so anger God that God ceases to be love. We cannot make God unjust. We cannot diminish God's beauty or deprive God of ultimate peace.

God's being personal is essential to our redemption from suffering. The forces that afflict us are often impersonal, and they wound us by denying our own personal significance. We are wounded by their indifference. God is never indifferent. One of the most troubling implications of the Casablanca model of suffering for spiritual growth (the idea that suffering in an impersonal universe is good because it teaches us that we do not matter) is that it portrays God as indifferent and calls our feeling insignificant "spiritual growth." That picture of an aloof God is utterly contrary to the Scriptural account of a caring God who values his people. God meets us personally at the point of our pain, and that is the beginning of our redemption.

GOD IS ETERNAL AND UNCHANGING

Once upon a time, a crow asked God to explain eternity. God said he would reveal eternity to the crow after it performed a task. The crow was to take a tiny piece of soil in its beak and fly away from the earth for a year, deposit its cargo and then return to repeat the process until he had moved the entire earth. So the crow set out to move a beakful of earth the distance of a crow's flight in one year. The crow did this, one beakful at a time, year after year, century after century, millennium after millennium, until it had moved the entire earth. The crow flew to God's throne and said, "I think I'm beginning to understand eternity." "You don't have a clue," God said. "Put it back."

When we say God is eternal, we are not just positing a possible characteristic that a being might or might not have. Eternity is at the heart of what we mean by the word "God." All things exist in time, and time exists within the context of eternity. But God does not exist inside any context larger than God-self. Eternity on the other hand cannot exist within God because, by definition, it is unlimited. God and Eternity have the same infinite dimensions. It might be said that eternity is a necessary truth, a reality we cannot deny, for if we posit a beginning to time, then eternity lies before that beginning; and if we posit an end to time, then eternity lies beyond that end.

When we say "God," we are saying something about the nature of eternity. We are saying eternity is beautiful and beneficent. That is what theologian Robert Jensen means when he says that religion is explicit seeking for eternity. When we understand eternity to be not just an abstraction but rather personal, then we call eternity "God."[29]

God is, by definition, limitless in time as well as space. The eternity of God makes God the source, foundation and context of all that is, "the Alpha and the Omega."[30] To say "God is eternal," however, is meaningful only if God is also unchanging. (Theologians call this doctrine "immutability.") Otherwise the God of today might be quite different from the God who first created us and quite different from the God who will be there at the end of time as our destiny. There are two sources for the traditional teaching that God does not change.

1. Scripture portrays God as steadfast, a steady character, dependable.

2. Greek philosophy thought change was an admission of defect, so God should never change.

It is not helpful or true to think of God as immutable in the sense of rigidity or endless repetition. A God who always thinks the same thought and feels the same emotion is not really personal. Is there any point in praying to a God who can't be moved? Scripture shows God being moved and changing his mind often. "Behold I am doing a new thing," the Lord said to Isaiah. The Jewish and Christian concept of God differs from that of Eastern religions in that this view of eternity does not cancel time by insisting nothing really changes, but rather presents eternity as open to transformation, which makes time meaningful.[31] The Christian God is an eternity in which change is possible. The Christian God holds open the door to hope for redemption. The Christian God's openness to story, to growth and to transformation is what makes our mortal human lives count.

The better way to understand the idea that God is unchanging is in the Hebrew terms of steadfast, dependable, faithful, committed love. God is always the dynamic personal love that constitutes the godhead, always compassionate, always creating, and always free to manifest in new ways. When we come to our study of the Trinity, we will see more fully that the eternal faithfulness of God is the foundation of our long term and ultimate hope to overcome evil and affliction. For now, just note this much: God is eternal. That which is not of God, that which resists God, for example, disease, injustice and cruelty, these things are transitory. In the end, there is only God. The unchanging eternal mercy of God ultimately conquers evil not by overwhelming it with power but by outlasting it with faithfulness.

God is love; God is beauty; God is just — when we are saying these things about God, we are describing the Alpha and the Omega. We are describing the very soul of eternity, that which will survive everything else and take the whole creation into itself. Suffering and death are not eternal. Only God is eternal. That means love, beauty, personhood — all the defining characteristics of God — are eternal. The eternity of God is the ground of our ultimate hope.

CONCLUSION

God is not a thing we can hold in our minds. God is vastly greater than our minds. So we naturally feel overwhelmed when we stop to consider who God is. Go ahead and be overwhelmed. That is the way to awe and reverence. To enter that sense of awe, stop now and consider that God is more loving, more beautiful, more just than we can imagine. Now remember that when we describe God this way, we are describing the very heart of reality everywhere and forever.

This is quite a different God from the dominator living outside the universe. If we replace that dominator image with the true defining characteristics of God — love, beauty, personhood — then we have a God who might want to do us some good. If we then say that this God is everywhere, near and far, eternal and unchanging, then all our troubles are set in quite a different context, a context laced with hope. Do you see how such a God might be the one to redeem our losses? All this is, as yet, pretty amorphous. It is just a beginning that can hopefully open the way to thinking larger thoughts about God. In the next few chapters, we will fold these vague characteristics of God into some actual images. These are images of God that have been largely forgotten by the modern world but like a long buried treasure, they may be just what we were looking for all along.

REFLECTION QUESTIONS

1. Are any of the God's characteristics described in this chapter new to you? Do any of them mean something different from what you had always thought?

2. If God were to change so as to lose any of these characteristics, would he still be God? Could God be unjust, unloving, mortal, limited to a single place, etc. and still be God?

3. Which characteristic of God do you think is most essential to God's being God?

4. If God exists and has these characteristics, how does God respond to human suffering?

NOTES

[1] Such a diverse lot as constructive theologian Gordon Kaufman, feminist theologian Sallie Macfague, Catholic transcendental theologian Karl Rahner, and liberation theologian Dororthee Soelle agree that our definition of God matters very much because God images shape who we become and determine our values.

[2] Quoted in Kenneth Leech, *True Prayer.* (San Francisco: Harper & Row Publishers, 1980), p. 3.

[3] Cheryl A. Kirk-Dugggan, *Refiner's Fire* (Minneapolis: Fortress Press, 2001), p. 156.

[4] I John 3 and 4, particularly 4:16.

[5] *The Book of Common Prayer*, in its various editions and adaptations, contains the order of worship for churches of the Anglican Communion. Archbishop of Canterbury Thomas Cranmer originally redacted it during the reign of King Edward VI. Cranmer drew most of the prayers from earlier liturgical texts. But the General Thanksgiving is his own composition.

[6] *The Book of Common Prayer* (New York: Church Publishing, Corp., 1986), p. 101.

[7] Douglas John Hall, *The Cross in Our Context: Jesus and the Suffering World*, (Minneapolis: Fortress Press, 2003), p. 22.

[8] Diogenes Allen, *The Path of Perfect Love.* (Cambridge: Cowley Publications, 1992) p. 15. Allen is drawing on Simone Weil's comments on Iris Murdoch's *The Unicorn.*

[9] Douglas John Hall, at pp. 98-99.

[10] David Bentley Hart, *The Beauty of the Infinite*, p. 177.

[11] Psalm 27:4; Zechariah 9:17; 1 Chronicles 16:29; 2 Chronicles 20:21; Psalm 90:17; John 17:24.

[12] David Bentley Hart, *The Beauty of the Infinite*, p. 195.

13 Hans Urs Von Balthasar, *The Glory of the Lord: A Theological Aesthetics* trans. Brian McNeil (San Francisco: Ignatius Press, 1989). David Bentley Hart, *The Beauty of the Infinite*. See generally, *Art, Theology, and the Church*, ed. Kimberly Vrudny and Wilson Yates (Cleveland: The Pilgrim Press, 2005). "Creation's being is God's pleasure; creation's beauty is God's glory; a Taboric effulgence, upon all things . . . that proclaims God's splendor . . . The delightfulness of created things expresses the delightfulness of God's infinite distance. For Christian thought, then delight is the premise of any sound epistemology: it is delight that constitutes creation and so only delight can comprehend it . . . " David Bentley Hart, *The Beauty of the Infinite*, pp. 252-253.

14 Adams, p. 147.

15 Cheryl Kirk-Duggan says the beauty of the divine image in the human soul draws us toward the contemplation of God's beauty in just this way: "If every human being is created *imago dei* [in the image of God], then (they creatively express) . . . holiness. That holiness . . . is resplendent in color, light, sound, fury, and love. Such holiness is beautiful and aesthetic. Aesthetics is a body of knowledge that comes from experiencing imagination, sensation, and the feeling of the idea of the beautiful. Beauty, along with truth and goodness, is a transcendental, a property that must accompany being and exists within every being. Beauty, therefore, is a path for the desire and longing that goes back and forth between God and us." Cheryl A. Kirk-Duggan, p. 155.

16 Romans 8: 18.

17 Adams, p. 155.

18 David Bentley Hart, *The Doors of the Sea*, pp. 88-89.

19 Elie Wiesel, *Night*. Trans. Stella Rodway (New York: Hill and Wang, 1960), pp. 70f.

20 Deut. 30: 11-14; Psalm 34: 18; Psalm 69: 18; Matthew 28: 20.

21 Isaiah 55: 9; Psalm 22:1; Ephesians 1:21.

22 Shirley Guthrie, at pp. 101–102. Patricia Fox, echoing Elizabeth Johnson and Han Urs Von Balthasar, says "Both theology and preaching often use God-language that is in fact too certain and distinct . . . YHWH signifies God's presence, not essence, and . . . the latter is unfathomable. Patricia Fox, *God As Communion*. (Collegeville: The Liturgical Press, 2001).

[23] John Hick, "An Irenean Theodicy," in Stephen T. Davis (ed), *Encountering Evil* (Louisville: Westminster John Knox Press, 2001), p. 42.

[24] "God as God, ground, support, and goal of all, is illimitable mystery who, while immanently present, cannot be measured, manipulated, or controlled . . . God's unlikeness to the corporal and spiritual world is total . . . it is proper to God as God to transcend all similarity to creatures, and thus never to be known comprehensively or essentially as God." Elizabeth Johnson, "The Incomprehensibility of God and the Image of God Male and Female," *Theological Studies* 45 (1984), pp. 441-442, Quoted in Patricia Fox, *God as Communion*. (Collegeville: The Liturgical Press, 2001), pp. 104-105. Johnson is drawing here on the writing of Hans Urs Von Balthasar, but is also expressing a general principle of Christian theology.

[25] See for example, Paul Davies, *The Mind of God*. (New York: Simon & Shuster, 1992).

[26] Simon Mawer, *The Gospel of Judas* (Boston: Little, Brown, and Co., 2000), p. 49.

[27] Simon Mawer, at p. 92.

[28] The personhood of God is part of the knowable God, part of the Job-Description Trinity. But the Family Trinity makes God personal even apart from his connection to us, indeed, makes the personhood of God intrinsic to his very Godness. So personhood pertains to the Transcendent God, to the Family Trinity as well. Karl Rahner insisted that the Economic (Job-Description) Trinity is the Ontological (Family) Trinity. He denied any radical disconnect in God between the Knowable God and the Mysterious. The Mysterious God is more than we can know, but is essentially like the God we know very well. Karl Rahner, at pp. 135-137. Martin Zizioulas' exposition on the personhood of God stresses that being a person is different from being an individual. He says that being a person is relational, that we are persons in relation to other persons. So the Family Trinity, as we shall see in coming chapters, expresses the eternal personhood of God. God is not

an individual. Nor do we speak of the three individuals of the Godhead, but rather of the three "persons" because they are constituted as persons by their relationship to each other.

29 A sense of eternity is essential to give our experience a context. Lutheran theologian Robert W. Jensen says, "human life is . . . 'meaningful' only if past and future are somehow bracketed . . . Thus in all we do we seek eternity. If our seeking becomes explicit we practice 'religion.' And if our religion perceives the bracket around time as . . . the possible subject or object of verbs — as in, for example, 'The eternal speaks by the prophets' — we tend to say 'God' instead of 'the eternal.' " Robert W. Jensen, *The Triune Identity* (Eugene: Wipf and Stock Publishers, 1982), pp. 1-2.

30 "Gregory (of Nyssa) understands 'infinity' when predicated of God . . . to mean . . . : incomprehensibility, absolute power, simplicity, eternity. God is . . . , elusive of every finite concept or act, boundless, arriving at no terminus: in Gregory's idiom, 'that which cannot be passed beyond.' " David Bentley Hart, *The Beauty of the Infinite*, p. 192.

31 Robert W. Jensen, p. 4.

CHAPTER 7

Dusting off an Ancient Riddle

I cannot believe that the inscrutable universe turns on an axis of suffering; somewhere the strange beauty of the world must rest upon pure joy!
— Louise Bogan

*There are things you cannot reach. But
you can reach out to them, and all day long.
    The wind, the bird flying away. The idea of God.
And it can keep you as busy as anything else, and happier. . . .*
— Mary Oliver, "Where Does the Temple Begin, Where Does It End?" from *Why I Wake Early*

THE ART OF GOD-TALK

We have made important headway by repudiating the image of God that makes the problem of evil intractable and blocks our way to a God who could do us some good. We have done necessary groundwork by saying a few things about what God is like. But the way we have been describing God is still woefully inadequate. It has been a list of adjectives, not a real image of God. It has been too abstract, just a cold naming of characteristics. We can know all these things about God without really knowing God at all. Popular Christian writer Robert Farrar Capon says:

> . . . [T]he first word in theology has to be not about God, but about the way we use words. Specifically, it has to be a firm warning that no words of ours can ever be trusted to mean the same thing when predicated of ourselves and God. Not even the florid ones with Greek and Latin roots. True enough, God is merciful and God is good, and

you may make him out to be as omnipresent, immutable and omniscient as you please. But never think for a minute that you have anything more than the faintest clue what it's actually like for him to be all those things.[1]

Talking about God is tricky. It requires a special language — language that can suggest something about the extraordinary truth of God, but not reduce it to something so simple we dare to presume we have got God figured out. Remember Augustine, "If you understand it, it isn't God."[2] We have made good headway, but we have not yet come to a way of talking about God that is particularly helpful when it comes to suffering. There is such a way of talking about God — a way of imagining God — that can sustain us instead of oppress us.

Joseph Campbell taught that the deepest, most important truths cannot be expressed directly. They cannot be described or explained in a straightforward way. The deepest, most important truths can at best be suggested, pointed toward, by stories and metaphors. Accordingly, the language of Christianity is not a literal description of God. It is a kind of divine poetry with God between the lines. The characteristics of God listed in Chapter 6 are all true and helpful to a degree — but they fall short of the image of God that is the heart of Christianity — the Holy Trinity.

In the next chapter, we will see why the Trinity is the key to understanding God's relationship with our suffering. But first, we need to understand a few things about the way we use language to talk about God. God is not ordinary so God-language cannot be ordinary either. If we try to use God-language as if it were ordinary language, we will find ourselves in an utter muddle and the beauty of this image will elude us.

ANALOGY, METAPHOR, AND PARADOX

The Tao that can be named is not the Tao.
  — Tao Te Ching

(A)ny God of whom an image can be made is shown thereby not to be the God of Israel.
    — Robert W. Jensen, explaining the Second
      Commandment, *The Triune Identity*

Doctrines describe God, not literally but poetically — theologians use the word "analogically." It has to do with the nature of God and the limits of language. We cannot put into words anything that is not first inside our minds. We cannot express in words everything we can conceive in our minds. Indeed, we cannot even find words for all the things we sense and intuit. God is vastly more than we can conceive. Trying to speak of God is almost an exercise in futility. Ludwig Wittgenstein[3] suggested that we should therefore "remain silent." Jacques Derrida[4] said we cannot speak *about* God, only *to* God. The God we can define with doctrines is not God. Yet, for several reasons, we *must* speak about God:

First, the experience of God compels us to speak. It is our nature to speak of what we experience; and we do experience glimpses of God. T. S. Eliot wrote of "hints and guesses." Like Jeremiah, we *must* speak of God. "If I say, 'I will not mention him or speak any more in his name,' there is something like a burning fire shut up in my bones. I am weary with holding it in. I cannot."[5]

Second, we are symbol-making creatures. Even ordinary experience calls for interpretation, and we interpret our world through symbols, including the ultimate symbol, "God," representing the source, destiny, meaning and order of all our experience.[6] By speaking of God, we strive to make sense of our lives and deepen our understanding. It is like making art. We grow in the process. Thought, reflection, and conversation enrich our experience by interpreting it.

Third, language about God sets the stage for us to experience God in ways we couldn't experience without that language. Cambridge theologian Nicolas Lash says that traditional images shape our current religious experience.[7] Rene Dupre' argues that we cannot have a religious experience until a symbol exists to open the door to that experience.[8] We interpret ordinary experience in religious terms, and those terms establish the foundation for future religious experience. Traditional images and concepts of God provide a structure of meaning. Without those images and models, we wouldn't be able to take in, grasp and interpret even our own experience. For example, Tibetans rarely have visions of the Blessed Virgin Mary because she is not part of their tradition. Conversely, Western Christians are not apt to have visions of Dakinis (dancing feminine spirits in Tantric Buddhism). Religious language, our symbol system, shapes and interprets experiences, which might otherwise go unnoticed.

Finally, we need language about God so we can talk to each other about our deepest values, so our religion will not be a private speculation, but a spiritual table at which a community can gather to support and sustain one another. Sigmund Freud disparaged religion by calling it a collective neurosis. But the psychoanalyst Eric Fromm retorted that neurosis is a private religion. Fromm is probably right. Religion becomes problematic when it is not rooted in community, and community is possible only with language. A faith community must devise a shared language of faith. Holy Scripture, sacred music, art, rituals and doctrines exist to give us a common language for sharing our religious experience.

Our dilemma is that we cannot speak about God, but we must speak about God. Rilke wrote,

*I want to utter you. I want to portray you
not with lapis or gold, but with colors made of apple bark.
There is no image I could invent
that your presence would not eclipse.*

The Christian way of dealing with the unspeakable reality of God — speaking only in metaphors — is very old. It is implicit in St. Paul, St. John the Evangelist, St. Gregory of Nyssa, and St. Augustine. Dionysius the Areopagite made it explicit in the 6th century. In his *Treatise On The Divine Names*, Dionysius set out an approach to theological language that has been the rule ever since. According to Dionysius, we cannot make any direct affirmative statements about God. God is simply beyond the reach of our language. It is impossible to say God is this or God is that. We can speak of God only by analogy, saying God is in some respect like this or like that. A medieval council of the Church affirmed that principle.[9] St. Thomas Aquinas endorsed it again. It persists today in the teachings of modern theologians such as Karl Rahner. The rule that we speak of God only by analogy is a settled, basic principle of Christian thought.[10]

But analogy does not mean two things are the same. It means they are somewhat alike and somewhat different.[11] For example, God is like a rock in that God is steadfast and dependable, but unlike a rock in that God is not hard, unresponsive, silicon-based and insensate. Moreover, in the case of God, Dionysius says, God is always *more unlike than like* whatever we are comparing God to. Whatever we say about God is more wrong than it is right. We need to say it anyway, but we need to speak reverently and humbly, acknowledging that we are stammering about something utterly beyond us.

Making statements about God is called the *via affirmativa*. Denying those statements is called the *via negativa*. The *via affirmativa* and the *via negativa* work together. We hold our claims about God in tension between saying God is sort of like this, but not really like this. God is love, but not like in a romance novel. God is just, but not like a human judge.

If we keep in mind that all our speech about God is analogical and not directly descriptive, it will save us from confusions that sometimes befuddle even good theologians when they get too caught up in their own imagery. A metaphor or image of God is intended to tell us something true about God. It will also invariably tell us something false. We must be careful to follow two rules: (1.) Do not extend the metaphor beyond its true point to include the false one. (2.) Do not discard the metaphor just because there is a false point that can be drawn from it. For example, when we call God "Father" we mean that God is our source and that God cares for us as a parent does. We do not mean that God is male.[12]

In addition to being analogical, the things we say about God are almost always paradoxical. Christian truth is often expressed as paradox, two claims that are logically contradictory, but both true. Paradox serves three purposes. First, it keeps us honest, keeps us from conclusively and absolutely saying things about God that are not quite right. Second, it keeps us reverent, prevents us from thinking we have God figured out. Third, it keeps our minds open because we cannot get them closed around a paradox. One of the great dangers in religion is fixed concepts about God. It is all too easy to close our minds around them. Any such concept would be an idol. Paradox keeps our hearts and minds open to the mystery.

When we discuss the Trinity, it will be crucial to remember that we are speaking analogically and that the paradox is deliberate. It will explain God only far enough to lead us into a mystery we cannot comprehend — but the Mystery can comprehend us and redeem us from deep wells of sorrow.

CLASSIC AND NEW METAPHORS FOR GOD

We have many traditional metaphors of God, mostly from Hebrew Scripture. God is a rock, a fortress, a parent, a mother bird, a king, a warrior, a storm, a volcano, an earthquake. Christians do not reject these pre-Christian metaphors; nor do Christians exclude the generation of new metaphors. Science sometimes provides metaphors. Scientist-theologian Pierre Teilhard de Chardin spoke of Christ as "the Omega Point" of creation, meaning our ultimate destiny. Chaos theory gives us the concept of the strange attractor who weaves the small-scale chaos of the world into large-scale order. The strange attractor metaphor suggests something of how God makes ultimate meaning out of events that seem meaningless at the time. Neuro-physicist Dana Zohar says, "The foundation of reality is a unified indeterminate maze of possibilities" — another good metaphor for the aspect of God that is the ground of our freedom. Jewish and Christian traditions have always used many names for God, names drawn from crafts and professions, the animal world, weather, and cosmic realities. No one metaphor can possibly capture the rich diversity and complexity of the divine nature — not even the Trinity.[13]

Theologians and philosophers use language about God that is not so obviously poetic as the Scriptural tropes, "rock," "storm," or "warrior." It sometimes sounds as if theologians are really trying to define God, but it is important to remember that they are not. For most of Christian history they have known better than that.[14] Theologians certainly know better than that today. Their concepts of God are poetic, metaphorical, partial expressions of our "hints and guesses." St. Athansius, the 4th-century Church father, like the 21st-century philosophical theologian Gordon Kaufman, emphasized that God is mystery.[15]

Doctrines are, to use a Zen metaphor, "fingers pointing to the moon." The danger the Zen metaphor illustrates is that we may find ourselves looking at the fingers, not at the moon toward which they point. Christians must be careful to hold our doctrines lightly, to let them direct our attention into the mystery.

Theologians have used many different expressions to suggest who God is — the cause and the purpose of reality,[16] the depth and meaning of everything,[17] our ultimate value from which all lesser values derive their worth,[18] Beauty, or the ultimate object of our desire, that for which we truly long from the very center of our souls.[19] "How late I came to love thee, O Beauty, so ancient and so fresh," Augustine prayed.

With so many ways of imagining God, is it any wonder that primitive peoples were often polytheistic? Monotheism makes the mind-boggling, soul-trembling claim that all these things are aspects of one transcendent reality — that our cause and our destiny are one with our highest value, our ultimate longing, our deepest meaning; that the highest good, the ultimate truth, and the greatest beauty are all one. Any single aspect of God can swallow us up in wonder and adoration. Yet, when we pull them all together, we still have merely hinted at a few of the easier aspects of God. Our metaphors — the explicit ones such as rock, fortress, parent or the ones that sound more like definitions such as "Ground of Being," "Unmoved Mover," "Transcendent Mystery" — are all metaphors. They are woefully inadequate to the reality about which we speak, but they are the greatest speech of which we are capable.

THE CLASSIC CHRISTIAN GOD-IMAGE

WHERE DID WE GET THE TRINITY?

The notion of Three In One is a conundrum we can't explain to anyone's satisfaction, not even our own. Oxford theologian Alister McGrath calls the Trinity "one of the most perplexing aspects of Christian theology."[20] Thomas Jefferson mocked it as absurd. It clearly was not designed to win converts. "It won't preach" — ask any pastor who's tried to explain it on Trinity Sunday. We wouldn't choose to create it. What's more, it's not in Scripture. The Bible gives us pieces out of which we construct the Trinity — but not a full-fledged doctrine of God in three persons with one substance, co-equal and co-eternal. The Bible doesn't compel the Church to adopt the Trinity as a way to imagine God. Where then did this difficult doctrine come from?

Some historians have told the story as if Trinity were arbitrarily made up and imposed by a Church hierarchy. It sounds like an outmoded dogma followed only by docile antiquarians. That story, however, is a gross distortion. At most the Church Councils refined and clarified beliefs that emerged from the worship and prayer life of the people, and had origins in both Christian and pre-Christian religious experience and thought. The sources of this image of God are rich and complex. Their roots are in the human spirit, not arbitrary decisions at Councils. The main tributaries into Trinitarian belief are Ancient Judaism; the struggle of the New Testament authors to explain Jesus; patterns of triads in other world religions; and finally the Early Church's experience of God.

There is a tension all the way back in the religion of Ancient Israel between the one God who is ultimately mysterious and the various ways in which this same God is intimately knowable. The unknowable sky God in Hebrew Scripture is called YHWH, El or Adonai. The knowable presence of God on earth is called God's Word, Spirit, Wisdom or Glory. Christianity inherits from Judaism this somewhat transcendent, somewhat immanent, somewhat knowable, somewhat mysterious, somewhat absent, somewhat present complex of God images.

The Jewish God is One (*Schema' Israel, Adonai elohanyu, Adonai echad* — Hear O Israel, the Lord your God is One) — but that does not make God simple. God is one in being, but multiple in actions and manifestations. In the Hebrew Scriptures God manifests in three-fold form as Wisdom, Word and Spirit.[21] Jewish monotheism was by no means Trinitarian, but it was not then, and is not now, simplistic. It acknowledges a certain diversity in God's ways of

Photo: Painting of the Trinity by Carol Alvarado / © Copyright Darrly Martin. Used with permission of both artists.

connecting with us. This diversity is analogous to what Christians call "modes of being." Ancient religion, which was generally polytheistic, was more aware of diversity within the Divine Nature than modern religion has been. The genius of Ancient Judaism was to look behind that multiplicity to find the unity.

The New Testament writers tried to explain Jesus using terms drawn from the Jewish tradition. Luke saw Jesus as special because he was filled with the Spirit of God. Matthew portrayed Jesus teaching the Wisdom of God. John and Mark understood Jesus as the personified Word of God.[22] In time, the Early Church developed the Doctrine of the Trinity primarily to say who Jesus is. The Trinity is the Church's effort to explain Jesus in terms of a God who is paradoxically hidden and remote, on the one hand; but close and intimate, on the other.[23]

It is common in the world religions to describe the Divine Nature in terms of triads. For example, in Buddhism, the center of reality is three movements called *kyas: dharmakya* (the natural order of things); *bodhikya* (the expression of the *dharmakya* in an awakened person); *nirmanakya* (the innate capacity in all sentient beings to wake up, to see reality as it is). In Hinduism major deities manifest in multiple ways. The great goddess manifests as a Triad, including a beneficent mother aspect, Parvati, and a threatening aspect, Durga (also called Kali). They merge into the more complex character of the goddess, Devi.[24] These triads are not the same as the Trinity.[25]

Nonetheless, the cross-cultural tendency to describe the Divine Nature with triad metaphors is part of the context in with the uniquely Christian doctrine of the Trinity arose.

Out of that rich background, Trinitarian doctrine was forged in the Early Church's lived experience as a eucharistic community. The Trinity expresses an experience of God among a group of people who celebrate Holy Communion on a regular basis.[26] But a eucharistic community shares more than ritual. It lives the bond of communion in daily life. The first Christians discovered a divine relationality in their relationships with each other. Encountering the Triune God through communion and community is the original Christian way of salvation. "Salvation," as the word was actually meant in the New Testament, does not mean to be pardoned for our sins, but rather to be made whole, to become fully human, to become a complete person. The first Trinitarians discovered that "to become fully a person . . . is to break through the isolating boundaries of individualism into a life of inclusive communion with persons valued for their uniqueness and differences . . . Arriving at full personhood in this way . . . is what it means to be saved."[27]

We did not choose the doctrine of the Trinity. We discovered it in the relational space between us. This God image emerges from life lived in communion and shared with a community of faith.[28] The image of God discovered in community was not of a dominating individual, but of a web of mutual appreciation and devotion. That is why the Christian God is not "the Supreme Being." If we believe power is what it's all about, we can use a powerful individual as a God-metaphor — perhaps a king, a general, or a C.E.O. That is the God who makes the problem of evil intractable, the big guy in the sky, the architect/contractor who made the world and now rules it with dominating power. We call it a Patriarchal God Image.[29]

An individual doesn't work so readily as a metaphor pointing toward the divine nature described in Chapter 6. For example, it is hard to picture God, the individual, being love when there was nothing outside God to love. We insist that God is one, meaning the divine nature is unified.[30] But God is bigger than any individual, even a very big individual, can represent. Our metaphor is the Holy Trinity. For those who want a nifty definition of God, it won't do. It is too complex, paradoxical and mysterious. But it invites us into a profound vision of how God responds to suffering.

THE TRINITY AS KOAN

Remember that the Trinity is deliberately a paradox. A paradox holds two opposite beliefs at the same time, which means one cannot hold either one of them very tightly. Christians claim that God is three and one at the same time. We may struggle to resolve a paradox as a way to break the mind out of the strictures of linear logical thought — like Zen students meditating on a koan (a riddle to which there is no rational answer). Meditating on a paradox breaks the mind free from the constraints of its own internal rationality in order to perceive reality in a direct way, not filtered through rationalist interpretation. The Trinity is intentionally mystical, outside rationality. It makes the mind spin into a state of reverence for God's unfathomable mystery. If we ever resolve the paradox so that the two beliefs cease to be opposites, then we have betrayed the very point of the doctrine.

In order to escape the discomfiting contradiction of a God who is one and three, we may lapse into saying God is really one, but seems to be three; or that God is really three, but they are so close that they seem like one. Either way of reducing the Trinity to something we can get our minds around betrays the paradox. Some theologians emphasize the one-ness of God; others emphasize the three-ness. But if either emphasis becomes too pronounced, it falls into heresy because it collapses the paradox and pretends to have solved the mystery.[31]

Christian faith insists on one thing about the Trinity, the paradox, which keeps us from grasping it. The paradox saves us from the irreverence of thinking we've trapped God within a box constructed of language. Irreverence consists in acting as if we know more about God than we do.[32]

SO WHAT'S WRONG WITH THE TRINITY?

You can learn a lot while drinking coffee in the student lounge of Harvard Divinity School. I was reading there one day when I overheard a conversation at the next table. Two young women, both on the verge of graduation, were discussing their futures. The first wanted to be a Congregationalist minister, but she didn't think the ministerial board would approve her. They would, she feared, expect her to believe in the Trinity — and she was not going to say that, no way, no how.

The other agreed that it was unjust and oppressive to expect her to affirm something like the Trinity. The first shook her head at the waste of her theological education and the cutting short of her ministry over such a thing. The second then said, "It's so seductive though, isn't it?"

"What do you mean 'seductive'?" the first asked.

"Well," the second said, "the way Prof. Coakley explains it, it's just so beautiful. It's about relationship instead of power as the heart of everything. It's really beautiful and so good, so moral."

The first student nodded and sighed, "Yes," she said, and when you read St. Basil and St. Gregory, and St. Thomas Aquinas, it just makes so much sense. It really seems true." There was a pause in the conversation. Then the first student continued. "It's hard to sacrifice all I've worked for on principle. But there's no way I'm going to say I believe in the Trinity."

"Of course not," the second student said. "It would be corrupt and absurd."

These were exceptionally bright people in their third year at Harvard Divinity. They knew full well that God is infinitely beyond any doctrine or description, that all doctrines are ways of using poetic language to reach into the dark, grazing the face of mystery with our fingertips. Why is this particular language about God, this particular sacred imagery, such a taboo that they recoiled against it no matter how beautiful, how good, and even how true it may be?

There is a deep resistance to the Trinity. It does no good to explain the Trinity, as long as this resistance is in place. So, let us start with the resistance. Most modern believers and unbelievers alike have the same definition of God, "the Supreme Being." First, God is a being. Second, he is supreme because he is supremely powerful. The Supreme Being is the cosmic patriarch. Some believe in this being. Others do not. But they agree on what it is they disagree about. The God they either believe in or do not believe in is a super-being with absolute power, who may be persuaded to do what we want if we will do what he wants.

That definition of God as the Master of the Universe is so unquestioningly assumed, that orthodox Christianity does not even make it into the conversation. I once watched an EcuFilm program featuring six contemporary Christian leaders speaking on the question "What Do We Mean By 'God'?" Neither the Trinity nor the Holy Spirit was mentioned — not even once in passing — and the Son was referred to only as the historical Jesus, not the eternal Word whom the Nicene Creed calls God. All six of the supposedly divergent viewpoints were stuck in the patriarchal god-image. Cambridge theologian Nicholas Lash says,

Under the dominant influence of modern theism, the doctrine of God's Trinity has . . . largely ceased to function as our Christian frame of reference.[33]

When many people say "God," they mean the patriarchal dominator. Even academic theology in the West often misses the ancient doctrine of the Trinity and lapses into a distinctly patriarchal heresy.[34]

To think of God as Trinity is to reject "modern theism." If God is the Trinity, God is not a powerful individual who dominates creation. Rather, God is a web of relationship, and this web does not dominate anything. It loves creation into being. This image of God is nothing short of revolutionary. So, in order to get beyond modern theism, we have to outgrow our childhood picture of God.

There are several reasons that people may object to the Trinity *on a conscious level*. They may never have heard the doctrine explained beyond simplistic metaphors to elucidate a metaphor. Many people often do not know that doctrines are metaphors pointing toward mystery, and that all religious metaphors are at best mixtures of truth and fiction. At the concrete literal level, the Trinity is simply non-sense. But beneath those conscious snags lies a cultural taboo. It is simply impossible to live in Western Culture without soaking up the mistaken definition of God as "the Supreme Being." That definition is a patriarchal culture's roadblock to grasping the Trinity.[35]

Remember our two theology students who praised Trinitarian doctrine in every way but refused to believe it. Why would sophisticated theology students — who decidedly know better than to think the Trinity is a silly polytheism, and who acknowledge that this poetic description of God is true, good, and beautiful — nonetheless resist it? Consider this statement: "I know it's a metaphor, not a literal fact. I find this metaphor to be true, good, and beautiful. But I refuse to believe it." Something deeper is going on.

Sigmund Freud make a huge contribution to religion by explaining the primary way we get this superman image of God stuck in our heads. It comes out of early childhood experiences of dependency. From the cradle, we learn that God is the patriarch, the monarch, the supreme boss, the dominator. We learn it psychologically in the family; then children's church school curricula and some patronizing clergy teach it as doctrine. It is doctrine — just not Christian doctrine — not Christian because the early childhood God image is not the Trinity.

If our parents were benign, we will feel safer with this dominator God. If our parents were frightening or neglectful, our attitude may be less positive. But either way, the universal condition of children is dependent and subservient. So we all learn the dominator God image from our primal experience of dependency on our dominator parents. It is the rare modern Westerner who does not have the patriarchal image entrenched in his or her assumptions about God, either consciously or unconsciously. If Freud is right — and I believe he is, *on a cultural level* — we all have the patriarchal God imprinted on our psyches. Certainly, each individual has his or her own personal history which shapes his or her own inner image of God, but as for the cultural norms that defines words, Freud was absolutely on the mark in describing the psychological foundation of a patriarchal culture's image of a patriarchal God.[36]

In a patriarchal culture, people will resist an anti-patriarchal God image and then generate conscious pretexts. Liberating one's religious imagination from the culturally imposed patriarchal-God trap is long, slow going. Reading this book will not be sufficient, but I hope it will help.

To be fair, we must acknowledge another reason for discomfort with the Trinity. We are deeply attached to thinking of God as an individual because it is easier to think of an individual as personal. It is easier to imagine an individual as caring, having opinions. It is easier to be friends with an individual.

When we say God is not an individual, people are apt to leap to the conclusion that God is not personal. That is 180 degrees opposite to the point of the Trinity. The Trinity image of God is the opposite of impersonal. It is more personal than an individual autocrat dominator-God could ever be. Personhood (feeling, thinking, hoping) occurs in the context of relationship. The Trinity shows God as essentially "interpersonal."[37] One might say the Trinity is at least three times as personal a God image as God the individual.

Granted, we cannot pray to a relationship.[38] But the Trinity itself, the godhead itself, the innermost being of God, is not the object of our prayer. We do not pray to the nameless, imageless God beyond our reach.[39] The three divine persons of the Trinity are, however, quite accessible in prayer. Jesus taught us to pray to the Father — not the godhead, not the divine nature. We pray to and through the Son. And we pray in the power of the Spirit. Trinitarian prayer is decidedly personal.

A final objection to the Trinity is that when we feel weak, we need someone to be strong. Being beautiful, good and true may be very nice. But when we are in danger, we want a cosmic Rambo to break down the door and save us. Yet the Trinity does not deny God's power. It changes *the nature of God's power*. God renounces dominating power but God still participates powerfully in our lives — there are forms of power other than domination. God's power is not the same as any other power we know. It is the power of creative love. God exerts power through relationship, personally, not oppressively — honestly, not manipulatively. Do we dare to believe love might be stronger than lightning bolts or assault rifles? This doctrine challenges our faith in domination. It might even change how we address the suffering in our own lives and the world. To describe God this way is to defy the power system religion.[40]

Trinitarian language isn't perfect. It suffers from regrettable gender bias.[41] But despite that clear problem, leading feminists theologians[42] vigorously defend the Trinity because it saves us from God as an individual — the big guy (and it is invariably a guy) in the sky. God as an individual is easy to understand — but the individual God usually becomes an autocratic power symbol, a king or a warrior. The Trinity makes God relational rather than domineering, interpersonal rather than abstract, egalitarian and mutual rather than oppressive. The Trinity portrays God as something like a spiritual force field in which the force is not dominating power but interpersonal longing.[43] The Trinity is not an adequate image for God. It should be supplemented by all the other metaphors from ancient tradition and new metaphors arising out of our culture. The Trinity is not adequate, but it is helpful, especially when we consider the problem of evil.

THE TRINITY FROM TWO ANGLES: TWO WAYS OF SEEING GOD THAT MAKE A DIFFERENCE

There are two fundamentally different models of the Trinity. Each of them tells us something different about how God responds to our suffering. I will label and define these two models in broad terms, before exploring in the coming chapters how they each express God's response to evil in the world.[44] The term "Job-Description Trinity" means this model is a picture of different roles God plays in relation to us. There is only one God — but this one God connects with us in three different ways.[45] God is like one person working three different jobs, each with its own job description. Taken all the way, this is an unacceptable way to describe the Trinity (that is, it is a heresy).[46] Taken all the way, the Job-Description model would destroy the paradox. But as a part of the description, it works fine.

The other model is the Family Trinity.[47] The three-ness of God here goes deeper than a job description. This Trinity is more like a family at home. "Home" here means what theologians call "the inner life of God." We might think of it as how God was before the Creation, when there was only God. The Family Trinity model says the inner life of God is already, actually and eternally relational. The Godness of God is a relationship among Father, Son, and Holy Spirit. That's what St. John means by "God is love." The three-ness of God extends all the way into the Godhead. Just as the Job-

Description Trinity, taken too far, is unacceptable, the Family Trinity, taken too far, is also unacceptable because it is too close to polytheism.[48] Taken too far, it would destroy the paradox. We hold these two models in tension, like a physicist trying to think simultaneously of an electron as both a particle of matter and a quantum of energy.

Remember, the Trinity is not a literal taxonomy of God. It is a metaphorical way of pointing toward what God is like. The two models actually describe God from different angles. The Family Trinity is an attempt to say how God is deep down, meaning what Reality is like at its very deepest level, what is the source of our being, what is the destiny of life. In a nutshell, the Family Trinity image is a way to say that God is interpersonal, that procreative love is the source of everything, and that such love is destined to be the consummation and meaning of history. The Job-Description Trinity is a way to say that God has three different ways of relating to us, different but complementary ways that work together for our well-being.[49] In the next four chapters, we will see what a world of difference this image of God will make for how we understand the human predicament.

CONCLUSION

In the face of tragedy, we ask: "why?" It is a theological question. Any answer must be couched in theological language. That language is not literal, factual, data-reporting. It is imaginative, evocative, poetic language. Part of our difficulty in making meaning out of our suffering is that suffering truly is mysterious. But modern people are utterly at a loss in the face of suffering because our modern concept of God is inadequate to the task. The dominator God metaphor makes the problem of evil intractable. The various explanations of evil we considered at the beginning were unsatisfactory because they were stuck in that bad metaphor.

In this chapter we have our first glimpse of a counter-image — a vision of God that breaks open the trap of patriarchal monotheism. We have met the ancient symbol of the Trinity — paradoxical in itself (three in one, one in three) and paradoxical in that it describes in different ways the inner life of God and how God relates to us. These two models, the Family Trinity and the Job-Description Trinity, are in fact the imaginative, evocative poetic language we need to respond to tragedy. They will not explain our pain away. They will not justify evil. Instead they will offer us a God of hope and provide a guide for how we can deal with our own heartaches and respond to the suffering of others. In the coming chapters, we shall see quite directly how both those aspects of the Trinity express God's response to our human predicament.

REFLECTION QUESTIONS

1. Which person of the Trinity do you pray to? Why that one? What might it be like to pray to another person of the Trinity?

2. Think of the explanations of the Trinity you have been taught. Were they more like one person with three jobs or more like three persons who were so close they were like one?

3. Does anything bother you about the titles "Father," "Son," and "Holy Spirit"?

4. Describe your image of God. Is your God-image more like an individual or a web of relationship?

5. How did you learn your image of God? How old were you when you learned what God is? Have you changed your image of God as you've gotten older? If so, how?

6. If you had to put your highest value — what you believe to be most important — into words how would you describe it? Does your image of God match your highest value?

7. Do you have any difficulty believing in the Trinity? If so, what makes it hard for you?

NOTES

1 Robert Farrar Capon, *Hunting the Divine Fox: Images and Mystery in Christian Faith* (New York: Seabury Press, 1985), p. 7.

2 Augustine, *Sermons 52*, Ch. 1, no. 16.

3 20th-century German linguistic philosopher.

4 Late 20th-century French deconstructionist philosopher.

5 Jeremiah 21:9.

6 Karl Rahner, at pp. 45-51.

7 Nicholas Lash, *Easter In Ordinary* (Notre Dame: University of Notre Dame Press, 1986), particularly at pp. 57-58 where Lash responds to William James' claim that authentic religious experience must be private and untainted by institutional or traditional faith, "Our 'private' experience is never entirely 'naked' . . . The symbolic, linguistic, affective resources available to us are given by prior experience, and by the culture, the traditions, the structures, institutions, and relationships that bring us to birth and give us such identity as we have. . . The innocent, naked, newborn 'ego' is a figment of the philosophical imagination."

8 "There is no religious experience prior to religious symbolization." Louis Dupre', *Symbols of the Sacred* (Grand Rapids: Wm. B. Eerdmans Publishing Co., 2000), p. 6.

9 The Fourth Lateran Council.

10 The idea that all speech about God is "analogous language" or metaphorical language is not just Dionysius' quirky idea. In 1215 CE, the Fourth Lateran Council instituted Dionysius' teachings about God talk as official Church doctrine. Great theologians from St. Thomas Aquinas to Karl Rahner have reaffirmed that language about God can only be analogy.

11 Alister McGrath describes analogy and metaphor as separate ways of describing God. However, they are the same in the one respect that

concerns us here. Both mean that God is somewhat like the image we use, and somewhat different. Alister McGrath, *Christian Theology* (Oxford: Blackwell Publishing, 2001), pp. 253-257.

[12] Alister McGrath, pp. 253.

[13] Patricia Fox. *God As Communion*. (Collegeville: The Liturgical Press. 2001), pp. 108-109.

[14] During the 18th and 19th centuries, faith was often considered to be a matter of propositional truths to be intellectually accepted. In that era, theologians often understood their own words more literally. But late 20th- and early 21st-century theology is acutely aware of the longstanding tradition that our speech about God is analogical, not literal.

[15] For Kaufman, God is the inherently unknowable aspect of reality — not just that which we have not figured out yet, but that which is always beyond our reach. Kaufman may go too far in equating God with the unknowable in that he gives too little emphasis to God's revelation, particularly in Christ. But Kaufman gives us a philosophically sound statement of the inherently mysterious quality of God. That mystery makes all our statements about God suspect if we take them as descriptions in the sense we might describes something we could truly comprehend.

[16] Thomas Aquinas

[17] Paul Tillich

[18] Karl Rahner

[19] St. Augustine and Hans Urs Von Balthasar.

[20] Alister McGrath, *Christian Theology* (Oxford: Blackwell Publishing, 2001), p. 319.

[21] Alister McGrath, p. 320.

[22] In Mark, Jesus is the one who speaks God's word, which is a creative force like the Hebrew *dabar*. In John, Jesus is God's word, which is the order of nature of reality, the Greek *logos*.

23 Alister McGrath, p. 322.

24 Gavin Flood, *An Introduction to Hinduism.* (Cambridge: University Press, 1996), pp. 174-197; Cornelia Dimmit and J. A. B. Van Buitenen, Classical *Hindu Mythology.* (Philadelphia: Temple University Press, 1978), pp. 220-226.

25 As Nicholas Lash says, "Trinities, triads, and triplicities are, indeed, found in many cultures, but most of them have little or nothing to do with the distinctions that Christians painstakingly elaborated in the attempt to safeguard what they had come to understand of the mystery of God considered in the light of Christ." Nicholas Lash, *The Beginning and End of Religion.* (Cambridge: Cambridge University Press, 1996), pp. 66-67.

26 Indeed Trinitarian language begins in the words of the liturgy, the language of worship, before it makes its way into creedal or confessional statements of the Church's beliefs. Jensen, pp. 10-12.

27 The words quoted are Patricia Fox's apt summary of Zizioulas, *Being as Communion*, pp. 49-50. Patricia Fox, *God as Communion* (Collegeville: The Liturgical Press, 2001), pp. 42-43.

28 John D. Zizioulas, *Being as Communion.* (Crestwood: St. Vladimir's Seminary Press, 1985), pp. 67-122. The hammering out of Trinitarian doctrine is a complex maze of struggle over metaphors and definition. See Jensen, pp. 57-159. The development of an orthodox doctrine of the Trinity is important and worthy of our study, but it makes the head swim more than is necessary for the purposes of this book. For our purposes, the important thing is to know that the Trinity is an image of God's personal relationality, that God is not an individual dominating reality, but a that God is Eternity whose inherent defining characteristic is love.

29 This book will be critical of "the patriarchal God." The criticism is not directed against the use of a Father God image in personal prayer and devotion. For some people, that image is a very helpful way to pray. Moreover, the Father is decidedly part of the Trinity. God as "Father," or "Abba" (actually the term of endearment used by Jesus to describe God) is a symbol of care and protection. God as "patriarch" is a symbol of domination and oppression. The Father God is not the problem. The patriarchal God is.

30 Monotheism is so deeply established in Western culture that we are apt to overlook what a bold leap of the religious imagination it is. To say that the source and destiny of reality are one with its meaning is not a given. To say that the greatest good, the truest truth, and the most beautiful beauty are all one is not a given. Monotheism combines a plethora of goods into one to generate the concept "God." That anyone should have thought such a thing, without inheriting the idea from others, is frankly astounding.

31 For a description of the heresies of modalism and tritheism, see McGrath at pp. 327-330.

32 Paul Woodruff, *Reverence* (Oxford: Oxford University Press, 2001), pp. 117-133.

33 Nicholas Lash, *Easter in Ordinary*, p. 277. Jurgen Moltmann argues that Western theology even at its best is predominantly heretical in terms of the Early Church statements on the Trinity. He examines Karl Barth as a representative Protestant theology and Karl Rahner as a representative Roman Catholic theology, and contends their views of the Trinity both amount to Sabellian modalism, a declared heresy essentially saying God is one individual performing three functions — the Job-Description Trinity taken to the extreme. If this is true of our great theologians, it is much more true of pastors in the pulpits and people in the pews. Western Christianity is out of touch with the richness of our traditional view of God. It is the feminist and liberation theologians who are reminding us of it.

34 Treating the Father as the real God, and the Son and Spirit as different ways in which the Father manifests, is essentially the heresy of Sabellian modalism. Moltmann rightly charges leading Western theologians including Schleiermacher, Barth and even Rahner with being essentially modalist. Sabellian modalism treats the Father as God the Commander, with the Son and Spirit as being either joint First Officer or more often as the First and Second Officer. They do not understand the Godhead as a network of relationship and so miss the feminist values of mutuality and compassion the orthodox Trinity represents.

35 Harvard Professor of Systematic Theology Sarah Coakley tells the story of a young woman studying for ordination in the United Church of Christ, perhaps the most liberal and least patriarchal denomination in the Christian tradition. She had grown up only minimally churched in that

liberal tradition and had never heard of the patriarchal image of God until seminary. She found the notion odd. But as she approached ordination, her dreams were filled with images of submission to patriarchal figures. Professor Coakley's point is that even those who do not consciously believe in such a picture of God are still subject to unconscious cultural influences.

36 Anna Maria Rizzuto's research in the psychology of God images showed that individuals form personal God images in more complex ways. Rizzuto, *Birth of the Living God*. But as a culture when we speak of God we necessarily adopt the culture's definition of God. Here I think Freud's understanding of our common God image is apt.

37 "The God who is a person is transcended by the God who is the Personal itself . . ." Paul Tillich, *Biblical Religion and the Search for Ultimate Reality* (Chicago: University of Chicago Press, 1955), pp. 13, 16, 24-26, 333-34, 59, 74, 82-84 generally explaining his thesis that God is personal without being an individual.

38 Notre Dame philosopher Robert Audi rightly observes that there is a problem with God's identity as relationship from the standpoint of religious practice and from the standpoint of Scripture. "One cannot pray to a relationship." The response to this problem is in terms of the two complementary albeit paradoxical models of the Trinity, which we will call the Family Trinity and the Job-Description Trinity. God in Godself is more like a personal relationship than an individual. But God, being relational, engages us in the personal manner we can be engaged. That is to say, God engages us in the form of persons — Father, Son, and Holy Spirit. Scripture is not a theological treatise on the nature of God. It is an account of God's interaction with people. So it tells the story in terms of the Divine persons whom we have met.

39 We may contemplate the imageless God in apophatic meditation. But petitions, intercessions and colloquies are to the persons to the Trinity, not to the mysterious Godhead.

40 The Trinity is not the only way to liberate ourselves from the dominator God. Nothing in Islam or Judaism, for example, preclude them from seeing God as relational. Martin Buber and Abraham Heschel are examples of such a view within Judaism. In Islam, the God of Rumi and al-Halaj is

no dominator. But the Trinity is Christianity's way of saying God is loving rather than domineering. The point in emphasizing the Trinity in this book is not to challenge non-Christian religions, which may have other ways of saying something similar about God. The point is to challenge a Christianity that, without the Trinity, has no effective way of saying that God is, at the core, relational rather than domineering. The relational, as opposed to domineering, nature of God is essential to a Christian understanding of how God and suffering fit in the same reality.

[41] Feminist theologians such as Elizabeth Johnson offer restatements of the Trinity in less patriarchal terms. On the other side, Robert Jensen defends the use of *masculine* language and argues it neither reflects nor supports patriarchal culture. Robert W. Jensen, *The Triune Identity* (Eugene: Wipf and Stock Publishers, 1982), pp. 13-16.

[42] For example, Sarah Coakley, Elizabeth Johnson, and Kathryn Tanner.

[43] The objection to talk about God in terms like "force field" (remember this is just an analogy) is that we don't think of a force field as personal. Actually, a force field may be more personal than we think. But to the extent that image connotes something impersonal, that is just the other half of the analogy. God is *like* a force field in size and energy, but *unlike* a force field in that God is personal.

[44] For a fuller account of these historical understandings of the Trinity, see McGrath at pp. 330-343. The Western Church leans toward the Job-Description Trinity. St. Thomas Aquinas called the Father, Son, and Holy Spirit modes of relationship — but the modes of relationship are within the Godhead. In other words, the Father is Father to the Son, and not just to the creation. Just so each person is defined in terms of relationship to the others. Three "persons" are not individuals — but subsistent relationships — like Fatherhood, Sonship, and Spirituality. Aquinas conceived God as a field of relationality. This field creates the universe and is its purpose and destiny. The Trinity is a visual image of the love at the center of reality which creates everything and is the meaning of everything, and therefore is the power that heals and redeems us in the midst of suffering. Theologians call the model of the Trinity that emphasizes how the one God relates to us in three ways or modes the "Economic" or "Modal" Trinity.

[45] "Job Description" is my own term, used to make the model clearer.

This model has traditionally been called the "modal trinity" or "economic trinity."

[46] This heresy is called "modalism." Alistair McGrath, pp. 327-328.

[47] St. Athanasius, one of the chief architects of the Nicene Creed's Trinitarian theology, compared the Trinity to a source of light, a ray of light, and illumination. Kathryn Tanner, p. 39. Theologians call it the "Social," "Immanent," or "Ontological" Trinity. The Eastern Orthodox Church emphasizes this model.

[48] David Bentley Hart, *The Beauty of the Infinite*, p. 169; Alistair McGrath, pp. 329-330.

[49] We should remember Karl Rahner's famous maxim "The economic trinity is the immanent trinity and the immanent trinity is the economic trinity." God's ways of engaging us are not unrelated to who God really is. Theologians who are willing to speak of the Family Trinity at all generally regard that as true. However, Hart cautions against two wrong ways to read this maxim. One is to make God's own nature and being dependent on the dynamics of creation's history and nature. This path leads to including the evil and violence of history in God's very nature, and so making them necessary. The other mistake is to forsake the Job-Description Trinity by disregarding God's revelation in the particular revelation of Jesus. David Bentley Hart, *The Beauty of the Infinite*, pp. 155-175.

CHAPTER 8

THE COSMIC VORTEX THAT SWALLOWS SORROW: HOW THE FAMILY TRINITY RESPONDS TO SUFFERING

O God, infinitely good and great, wonderful indeed are the truths that faith lays open to us, concerning the life which Thou leadest within Thyself; and these truths dazzle us.... Your joint ecstasy leaps forth the strong flame of love.... You alone, O adorable Trinity, are the interior life, perfect, superabundant, and infinite. Goodness unlimited, You desire to spread this, Your own inner life, everywhere outside Yourself.[1]
— St. Augustine, *Sermon 2 de Nativity*

THE FAMILY TRINITY IS A DANCE OF LOVE

St. Gregory of Nazianzen and St. John of Damascus described the Family Trinity, the inner life of God, as a *perichoresis*. *Peri* means "around" as in "perimeter" or "perambulate." *Choresis* means "a dance." The Trinity means that God is like a circle dance, such as a Native American, Middle Eastern, or Mediterranean folk dance.[2] T. S. Eliot wrote in his poem, *Burnt Norton*:

At the still point of the turning world...
at the still point, there the dance is...
Except for the point, the still point,
There would be no dance,
And there is only the dance.

Hinduism describes the divine nature as the cosmic dance; and here, in the doctrine of the Trinity, the dance serves as the metaphor for the foundation of reality. Reality is, at its heart, a community, a striving for relationship. For contemporary feminist theologians, *perichoresis* signifies the ultimate value of mutuality in relationship.[3] This dance of God is the foundation of everything beautiful in creation.[4] The circle dance of the Holy Trinity, is a metaphor of the "pure joy" on which "the strange beauty of the world must rest." The Trinity is a way of imagining an axis of joy, or mutual delight and love, which is the foundation of all creation. In this chapter we will explore how that joy, love, and beauty can heal and restore us from even horrendous evil and suffering.

Augustine was less metaphorical. Instead of describing the Family Trinity as a dance, he explained it in terms of love.[5] We will freely paraphrase it here so that we can more readily revise it to make it more helpful. The first person of the Trinity is the Lover. In order for the Lover to be the Lover, there must be an object of his love. The second person of the Trinity is, therefore, the Beloved. The Lover makes the Beloved "beloved" through actively loving. The Beloved makes the Lover "Lover" through passively being loved. The spontaneous response to such perfect love, however, is to return it. The Beloved becomes the Lover; and the Lover becomes the Beloved. Between them flows the love, and that love is the third person of the Trinity, the Holy Spirit.[6]

Lover-Beloved-Love is an engaging way to express the nature of God. However, there is a problem. The Lover sounds personal; the Beloved sounds personal; but the Spirit sounds like a feeling they have. The Spirit sounds secondary and not quite personal. It does not have a face.[7] To overcome this problem, we might think of the Spirit as being like Puck, the wood sprite in *A Midsummer Night's Dream*. Puck sprinkled magic dust in the eyes of young people sleeping in the forest to make them fall in love. We might think of the Spirit as the instigator of love between Lover and Beloved.[8]

There is one distinction we must make though. Puck's magic dust caused Shakespeare's lovers to see each other through a fog of illusion. The Spirit, on the contrary, enables Lover and Beloved to see each other clearly as they truly are and so instills love rooted in reality. Put just a shade less metaphorically, one might say the Love arises in the relational space between the other two, and in arising, bestows on them their identities as Lover and Beloved. The Lover exists as Lover only by loving the Beloved, and the Beloved exists as Beloved only because of the Lover's love. Puck is as essential to their

being as they are to his. The Spirit Puck is as personal as the other two; as active a player in the divine love story out of which everything is born, in which everything has its meaning.[9]

"At the heart of holy mystery is not monarchy but community; not an absolute ruler, but a threefold *koinonia* (partnership)," says feminist theologian Elizabeth Johnson.[10] God is the communion out of which all things are born and in which all things find their destiny. Instead of representing our highest value with an oppressive power, the Trinity shows our highest value as a love story. We grow to be more like our image of God. The patriarchal God calls us to become more patriarchal, to claw our way up the ladder of power, to excel in one-upmanship. The Trinity calls us to life in community, in interpersonal relationships of caring mutuality.

The central point of the Family Trinity image is that God is a network of love. That ancient insight is the key to understanding how God responds to our calamities. Out of love, God creates and holds in being everything that exists. This is vast power — but it is not the literal omnipotence of an autocrat. Literal omnipotence is the power to impose one's will by fiat and force. God does not have that kind of power and could not exercise that kind of power and still be the relational God. But God does have another kind of power far beyond

Photo: Spiral galaxy M81. / © NASA, ESA, and The Hubble Heritage Team (STScI/AURA). Used with permission.

the reach of our imaginations. God's vast power is the power of love, sometimes suffering love.¹¹ God's love is compelling, not manipulative or coercive. It compels by its own beauty and attraction. There is a crucial difference between the power to impose one's will by force and violence, on the one hand, and the power to give birth, to attract, or to heal, on the other.

This is a variation on the "free will defense" — but it is an important variation. In the classic "free will defense," the literally omnipotent dominator God deigns to allow free will because he decides it will be "better for us." He could have made a different choice and he can call the deal off anytime he chooses. But the God whose very nature is relationality would not and *cannot* — I will not hedge on this — *cannot* create a puppet universe. Such a God would not and cannot dominate the universe. That dominance would be contrary to God's own nature. Moreover, it would deprive the universe of the autonomy that is essential to our capacity for genuine relationship with God and each other. That model would deny the existence of both the Creator and the Creation, as we understand them. But the Trinitarian/relational God I am describing would not and could not fail to love and redeem the Creation. That is the ground of our "sure and certain hope."

THE FAMILY TRINITY AS PARENT

As we have seen, the reason we describe God as Trinity instead of an individual cosmic monarch is to show that God is not a dominating power but a loving creative influence. Instead of starting our question about evil and suffering with the picture of an architect/contractor designing and building a flawed universe, we start with the belief that at the core of reality is an interpersonal field of relationship like a family. Love is at the heart of things.

The persons of the Trinity freely choose to love each other.¹² That cosmic love does not design and construct but rather *procreates* the universe.¹³ Notice the role of freedom here. Love depends on free will. The universe is born from this divine free will to love. The creation is not identical to God any more than children are identical to their parents. But something of the parent is invariably present in the child. Just as God is personal, the universe is personal. It longs for relationship. Modern physics has shown this personal quality, this relationality and will, manifest even in sub-atomic particles.

They do not merely bounce about mechanically like billiard balls. Rather, they dance in relationship with each other. We see it in the eco-system and the order of heavenly bodies. We see it most clearly in human beings in relationship with one another. Because we are created in the image of God, we long for relationship.

Yet, the universe is imbued with freedom, as the heart from which it is born is a free heart. The free will of the universe can and sometimes does reject relationship. Because relationship is freely chosen, it is personal rather than mechanical. We have to be able to say "no" to love if our "yes" to love can be love itself and not a mere reflex. Suffering and evil arise from rejection of relationship.

Since God is love, we cannot attribute suffering to either divine malice or divine indifference. If God were malicious or indifferent, God would not be God. God's response to suffering and evil is not malicious or indifferent. God's response is loving and faithful. But how does that work?

HOW THE TRIUNE GOD RELATES TO OUR SUFFERING

INVOLVED WITHOUT DOMINATING

The Family Trinity model of God makes relationality, including compassion, the very essence of God. If God were not compassionate, then God would not be anything at all. God would not be. If God is compassionate, then God suffers with us. As the hymn says,

> "There is no place where earth's sorrows
> are more felt than up in heaven."
> — Hymn 469 by Federick William Faber,
>   The Hymnal 1982 (Episcopal)

As any parent longs to ease her child's suffering, God longs to ease our suffering. Jesus said as much, "Which of you when his son is hungry will give him a stone instead of a fish? If you who are evil know how to give your children good things, how much more does your Father who is in heaven?"[14] God wants us to be happy, as a parent wants her child to be happy. God wants to ease our suffering.

If God wants to ease our suffering, then why doesn't God do it? Let's stay with the parent image a bit longer. There are times when a good parent could solve the child's problem, bail him out, pay his fine, but the good parent has to let a child suffer in order to grow and learn. There are other times when the suffering is simply not in the parent's power to overcome. (I write this after meeting with a father whose 26-year-old daughter has just been diagnosed with aggressive cancer. As we go to press, I have just officiated at her funeral mass.) Both of those situations may arise for God. Such factors as natural law, our mortality, and free will may prevent God from simply alleviating suffering with the wave of a hand.

Can a God who is not literally omnipotent do us any good? Yes, definitely so. Although God allows the universe freedom, that does not mean God has nothing to do with it. Although God does not dominate the creation, God is still engaged with it, using the power of faithful love instead of the power of domination. God is intimately present in all situations.[15] God is here in the midst of everything. "The kingdom of God is within you." But God is present as the Trinity of Love, not the dominating patriarch. God is present not as a ruler, but as a guiding parent, as a healer and a friend.

The doctrine of the Trinity means that God is a whirlpool of love, a vortex of relationality, drawing the world into God's-self, luring the whole creation and each of us as individuals into participation in the divine nature, which is Trinitarian love. God invites — but does not compel — peace and healing. And God is by and large amazingly successful. The world really does function at an extraordinary level of truth, beauty and goodness. On a given day, perhaps bombs explode in Bagdad. That is tragic. But on that same given day, no bombs explode in Cairo, Belfast, Sarajevo or Johannesburg, and that's practically a miracle. There are many such days. In ordinary and extraordinary ways, the lure of God and the innate godliness of the world make miracle and wonder.

So God does not dominate; but God does exercise influence. We haven't a clue as to what determines when and how God acts more palpably, while at other times, God's influence is not nearly as strong as we wish. The general limitation is that God must allow the universe autonomy. But this barrier to grace is not absolute and it can be shifted or thinned out by prayer and human action in cooperation with grace. To the extent that the world does not freely submit itself to God, the world eludes somewhat God's gracious mercy. When we submit to God in prayer and action, we draw the world with us into a nearer communion with its source. We become a channel of grace. This is not to say God is utterly unable to help us even if, hypothetically, no one on earth were praying or had ever prayed or ever would pray. But it is to say that someone praying sometime somewhere opens a wider path for mercy, disposes the world more toward grace.

God wants nothing more than to work graciously in the world, but there is a line God cannot cross — uninvited — without infringing upon the autonomy of creation. We are part of creation and we are connected to all of creation. By virtue of being part of all creation, we have some (not complete, but some) authority to move that boundary line, to invite God in. Our submission to God in prayer is both on our own behalf and on behalf of creation. God will not act beyond a certain point without permission from us, but God has authorized us to give that permission and has implored us to give it.

God's action and our freedom work in a subtle tension. We more or less choose our own actions in freedom, albeit our freedom is constrained by the powers and principalities of the world. Moreover, we are quite unable to control the consequences of our actions. Sometimes well-intended actions turn out badly due to randomness. But often, God weaves the unexpected consequences of even sinful acts and tragic accidents into grace or goodness.

Scripture tells the wonderful story of Joseph, who was sold into slavery by his brothers but became the chief officer in charge of all the wealth of Egypt. His brothers came to Egypt during a famine, hoping to buy grain. When they realized who Joseph was, they were naturally afraid that he'd take his revenge. But Joseph explained that despite their evil intent, God had used the whole ugly story for good, to preserve life.[16] Despite our moral frailty and general incompetence, just as a Strange Attractor brings order out of chaos, Something or Someone often brings good out of the unforeseen consequences of our actions.

HOW GOD ACTS IN THE WORLD

Believing *that* God acts might be easier if we could get a little more clarity on *how* God acts. Bart Ehrman refuses to believe in God because he understands God as one who "intervenes" in our lives to prevent bad things from happening — but he doesn't see the interventions. The idea of *intervention* assumes God is outside the situation to begin with, then jumps in and takes over. But God is already involved in the mix and the muddle of life, albeit in a loving way — not a dominating way. So how does the Christian tradition see God's hand at work in the world?

There are three basic models for how God participates in our world. First, there is the *Deist view* that God does not act in a personal or deliberate way. God's presence is only though the existence of *natural laws*, which are on the whole beneficent. Second, there is the *classical view* espoused by Thomas Aquinas that God does not act directly to cause anything specific. Rather God acts through *secondary causes*. To the extent things go badly, it is the fault of the secondary causes. Finally, *process theology* maintains that God does not cause specific events to happen. Rather God *influences* all events, luring them toward the ultimate purpose, toward the true destiny God intends.[17]

The Deist and process views are fairly clear but the classical view is couched in language a bit foreign to us. It may be helpful to offer some examples. "Secondary causes" would include actions of people who freely choose to obey God's will. A nun bathing the wounds of a leper is a secondary cause because she is obeying God's will. The leper receives mercy through a secondary cause, the nun. God's word speaking to the nun may also have been mediated through another "secondary cause," such as a teacher or the scripture or the examples of saints, but there may also have been a more direct spiritual experience, a felt sense of call. That experience may be a "direct cause." In the classical view, God may directly cause general things like someone's gentle character. But specific events, like acts of mercy, come through secondary causes.

Sometimes the hand of God seems more active than at other times. Regardless of how God acts, divine causes must always be understood as essentially *influencing* rather than *dominating* events. The Deist, the Thomist (classical view), and the process theologian all agree on that much. God participates in our lives, but there is a line God does not cross, and logically cannot cross, without infringing on the autonomy of the creation, without turning the creation into an extension of God rather than an independent reality capable of personal relationship with God. Exactly where that line is we cannot usually say. But God sees it and will not cross it.

DISCERNING GOD'S WILL

It would be so simple either way — to say that whatever happens is God's will or to say that God's will has nothing to do with how things go. Either view would relieve us of having to think very much. But if some things that happen are God's will and others are not, then we have to pay attention and try to discern, albeit imperfectly. In thinking about the role of God's will in human affairs, there are several more categories it will be helpful to remember.

We have already distinguished between God's *active* and *permissive* will. God actively exercises influence to bring about good. He permits the world to be other than he would choose, and that leaves room for evil. It also helps to distinguish between God's *primary* and *secondary* will.[18] God's primary will is that we do good deeds and flourish. Since the creation is substantially free, however, God's primary will all too often does not come to pass. God's secondary will is the good that God weaves out of the unintended consequences of our bad actions and the bad things that befall us. It is, in other words, God's Plan B. The universe runs largely according to God's Plan B or even C. Plan A was better, but Plan B will get us through until the end times when all things find their destiny in God.

The surprising grace of God's bringing good out of evil does not justify the sin or tragedy. I am not citing this grace as a justification of anything. I am merely saying how God works in the weather of human life. We make plenty of our own clouds. The nature of mortal life makes clouds aplenty. God is not a manufacturer of clouds. God makes the silver linings.

Finally, it may help to remember the distinction between God's *general will* and *specific will*. As an example of specific active will, God may act to bring about some precise good — but through influence, not coercion. For example, God may call Mother Teresa to serve lepers in Calcutta. God's broad desire for the flourishing of creation is general and active. Without any specific plan for how this is to happen, God rejoices in and encourages the good including beauty, peace, and justice. God's will to allow the creation freedom is *general* and *permissive*. This freedom is the space in which both good and bad things happen. There is no credible argument for God's active will to bring about any specific evil.

THE BASIS FOR HOPE

What then can we actually expect God to do for us? From the spiritual vantage point of St. John of the Cross, or the lofty philosophical perspective of D. Z. Phillips, we must truthfully say that we are called to love God for being God — not for anything God can do for us. However, we are human and all too often in desperate need. Then the question of what God can and will do for us cannot be brushed aside by either mysticism or philosophy. We need to know what we can expect of God.

Moreover, our longing for God to be a Savior and Redeemer is not inherently selfish.[19] Leave our personal needs out of the equation. A child dies of poverty or a preventable disease every three seconds. We expect God to do something about that, or at least to want to do something about that. If God is not responsive to the suffering of creation, then is this God lovable? Setting our own needs aside, we still insist that God must be a Savior and Redeemer in order to evoke our love. Indeed being a Savior and Redeemer is part of the definition of divinity, a criterion of what we worship, a key element of what we mean by the word "God." God, in order to live up to the name of God, must be willing and able to offer us hope.

Our Family Trinity view of God gives rise to two distinct forms of hope — *short-run hope* for good to prevail here and now in the affairs of this world and *long-run hope* that in a future beyond our view all will be well. The short-run or immediate hope is this: There is no situation in which God is not active, working for peace, justice, and healing.[20] That is part of what we mean by the doctrine that God is everywhere, including right here with us. Because God is present in every situation, there is always hope. *Expecting* miracles, as Robert Schuller prescribed, is naive. By definition, miracles usually do not happen. You cannot expect them. *Hoping* for miracles, however, is a natural expression of a reasonable faith. We acknowledge that there are limits to what God can do in our affairs, but we do not know what they are. Scripture and experience abound with God's surprises of saving and healing grace. There is always hope for something good. Indeed, good things often happen. Sometimes glorious things happen, occasionally miracles.

Our ultimate hope, however, is in the long run. Christian faith offers healing and reconciliation now, but on a partial and temporary basis. Everyone Jesus healed eventually died. Our real hope is resurrection hope. Our ultimate hope lies in a world to come.

What is the ground of that hope? Although the universe has freedom to defy God, that freedom does not put the universe and God on equal footing. God is still creator and we are still creature. The difference between the Creator and the creature is that God's persistent love lasts for eternity. All that resists God is mortal, and therefore ultimately futile. Human souls created in God's image are neither useless nor futile, but eternal and blessed. The forces that resist God's love, however, are futile. Those forces are such things as death, disease, cruelty, injustice, and prejudice. God wins, not by force but by persistence through eternity. That's the meaning of God's unchanging faithfulness. Because God's persistent love lasts for eternity, our ultimate hope is assured. All God has to do in order to redeem the whole creation is simply to remain God and wait.

Ocean waters are swept along temporarily by waves, swells and tides. But deeper currents, like the Gulf Stream, determine the waters' long-run course. God's faithful love for creation is the deep current in reality, the current that will eventually carry us home. When we arrive home, we finally see God. "For now we see in a mirror dimly, but then face to face. Now I know in part; then I shall understand fully, even as I have been fully understood."[21] Marilyn McCord Adams defends this hope in her argument that the beatific vision of God's beauty will in eternity redeem even the horrendous evils that can never be justified or explained.[22]

If our ultimate hope lies in God's eternal persistence and in the final futility of all that resists God, does this lead to universalism, the claim that God's salvation is not for a chosen group, but for all? Gregory of Nyssa's answer was "yes."[23] While much Christian tradition insists on a final division between good and evil, theologians such as Origen as far back as the 3rd century insisted that the nature of God assured us of the final redemption of the entire creation.

CONCLUSION

The Family Trinity is an image of the basic nature of God's creating and redeeming love for us. There are two kinds of hope in the Family Trinity: short term hope based on our faith and experience that God is involved in every situation, not dominating and controlling it, but influencing and luring it toward the highest possible good; and long term hope in our trust that God alone is eternal and in God's eternity all shall be more than well, all shall be healed, redeemed and glorified.

However, when I have said God is present in all situations working for our good, I have been rather vague. In the coming three chapters on the Job-Description Trinity, I will clarify how God acts in the midst of our hardships. God reaches out to us in three distinct ways to help us with suffering. The Job-Description Trinity represents these three fundamental ways in which God touches us and responds to human affliction. In the next chapter we will consider the response of the Father.

REFLECTION QUESTIONS

1. Have you ever danced a circle dance? What was it like?

2. What is your reaction to hearing God described with words like "Lover," "beloved," "Puck," and "circle dance"?

3. What difference does it make to our understanding of the ways of the world if God is a field of relationality instead of an architect/contractor?

4. Theologians sometimes speak of the "permissive will" of God as opposed to the "active will" of God. Can you think of why God might permit something God would not actually cause? Are there things you would permit others to do, but you wouldn't compel them to do? In attributing responsibility for suffering to God, does it matter whether God causes it or permits it?

5. Can you think of ways God might be involved in a human situation without controlling it? How might God influence the course of events without overriding freedom?

6. What do you believe happens to the universe in the end? What do you believe was before the universe? Will reality be different after the universe ceases to exist in its present form?

NOTES

1 *Factus est homo ut homo fieret deus.* St. Augustine, *Sermon 2 de Nativity*, quoted in Dom Jean-Baptiste Chautard, *The Soul of the Apostolate* (Garden City: Image Books, 1961), p. 23.

2 Alister McGrath, *Christian Theology*, pp. 325-326. Presbyterian theologian Shirley Guthrie was closer to John of Damascus than to John (Calvin) of Geneva. Guthrie wrote, "The oneness of God is not the oneness of a distinct, self-contained individual; it is the unity of a community of persons who love each other and live together in harmony." Shirley Guthrie, *Christian Doctrine.* (Louisville: Westminster John Knox Press, 1994), p. 92. That is a good statement of the Family Trinity — except that the three "persons" aren't distinct self-contained individuals either. The whole imagery of persons is not about distinct individuals. Rather, it is a way of saying that the nature of God is personal or, better, interpersonal. God's nature can best be pictured as analogous to interpersonal relationship.

3 Patricia Fox. *God as Communion* (Collegeville: The Liturgical Press. 2001), pp. 140-142.

4 "The Christian understanding of beauty emerges . . . from the Christian understanding of God as a *perichoresis* of love, a dynamic coinherence of the three divine persons, whose life is eternally one of shared regard, delight, fellowship, feasting, and joy. . . (God's) beauty possesses the richness of every transition, interval, measure, variation — all dancing and delight. And because he is beautiful, being abounds with difference: shape, variety, manifold relation." David Bentley Hart, *The Beauty of the Infinite* (Grand Rapids: Wm. B. Eerdmans Publishing Co., 2003), pp. 155, 177.

5 We are dealing here with only a fragment of Augustine's Trinitarian doctrine because the full doctrine is more complex than is helpful for our purpose of understanding God's connection to suffering. In a simplistic nutshell: Augustine looked into human nature to learn about God. Augustine found in the human soul an inner Trinity of Memory, Reason and Will. He took this tri-partite human soul to be a mirror of the Triune God. Father, Divine Mind, and Spirit manifested these same aspects of soul in God. He distinguishes between the Family Trinity and the Job-Description Trinity in this respect — In the Family Trinity, each person is co-equal and co-eternal, but in the Job-Description Trinity the Father comes first; then the Son and

Spirit appear later on the stage where our salvation is worked out. McGrath, pp. 331-332.

6   Alister McGrath, *Christian Theology*, p. 332.

7   Alister McGrath, p. 332. This is a simplified way to state the traditional Eastern Orthodox objection to the Western Augustinian model of the Trinity, that it fails to represent the Holy Spirit as a truly separate person rather than as roughly the same as the godhead itself. See, Geoffrey Wainwright, "The Holy Spirit" in *The Cambridge Companion to Christian Doctrine*, ed. Colin E. Gunton (Cambridge: Cambridge University Press, 1997), p. 292.

8   This Puck metaphor expresses David Bentley Hart's point that the Spirit is more than a bond of love. The Spirit breaks the other persons of the Trinity open to each other. It is causative of their relationship, not secondary to it. David Bentley Hart, *The Beauty of the Infinite*, p. 176.

9   This Puck metaphor, like all divine metaphors, is flawed. The doctrine of co-eternity insists that all of this happens simultaneously. This metaphor is also flawed because it obscures the doctrine of "procession." But that's a more tricky doctrine than we need to explore for our purposes. It also leads down a slippery slope into the *filioque* controversy between the Eastern and Western Church, a controversy that definitely sheds no light on our problem of evil.

10   Elizabeth Johnson. *She Who Is* (New York: Crossroad, 1992), p. 216.

11   Stanley Hauerwas is a leading contemporary example. This notion is at home in process theology and philosophy represented by Charles Hartshorne, the liberation theology of Jurgen Moltmann, and early 20th-century Anglican theology, represented by C. E. Rolt. Adams, pp. 70-75, 159-160. The power of "suffering love" could be problematic if it is understood as the power of suffering as a way to manipulate others with guilt. But Paul Tillich argued that love is inherently powerful in its own right. He noted Nietzsche's argument that the will to power is superior to Christian love. But the power Nietzsche extolled was not the power of control and domination, but rather power as the force of life and creativity. Paul Tillich, *Love, Power, and Justice* (London: Oxford University Press, 1954). And the "Christian love" Nietzsche rejected was a pusillanimous sentimentality, not a life-generating force.

12 This is a point at which our metaphor stumbles a bit. In Eastern Trinitarianism, with its emphasis on the three-ness of God, it sounds as if we are saying each person of the Trinity has a separate will independent of the other. Kathryn Tanner rightly says that idea misconstrues the meaning of "person" in the ancient creeds, and that God must have unity of will. She is clearly right. But I don't think we need to take the metaphor of the Family Trinity so literally. It is a metaphorical way of saying there is relationality in God and that relationality is exercised in freedom rather than necessity. One needn't imagine that the Father would opt for love while the Son would reject it. The point is just that God, in freedom, chooses relationality rather than splitting and conflict.

13 This argument does not mean that God has to create the universe. This would mean the universe is necessary, that God becomes Godself only in relation to the universe. That is not my point. Since God's nature is procreative love, it is natural that God would create the universe and natural that God would create the universe in freedom. But it does not follow that God has to do so. God could remain relational entirely within the Trinity. Part of the beauty of the doctrine of the Trinity is that it portrays God as relational without being contingent on anything other than God with which to have a relationship; but it also portrays God in such a way that creation is a natural outpouring of the Divine Nature. David Bentley Hart, who is quite insistent that God's act of creation is voluntary and gratuitous, "that creation is without necessity," allows that "it has been from eternity fitting to God's goodness to be a loving creator, manifesting his trinitarian love in creatures." David Bentley Hart, *The Beauty of the Infinite*, p. 256.

14 Matthew 7: 9-11.

15 Some of the best thinking on the Family Trinity's connection to suffering is from Elizabeth Johnson in *She Who Is*. Patricia Fox in *God as Communion* aptly summarizes her argument at pp. 135-157. Johnson's approach deserves more than a footnote, but I am addressing it in this cursory way because dealing with it more fairly would draw us off course. Johnson argues for a relational Trinitarian God who suffers with the world, but suffers in generative power, like birth giving, and exercises power with the world rather than over it. I find her argument persuasive but I would like to see two points better developed. Her portrayal of God is primarily immanent. I am not sure how God, as Johnson sees God, can stand outside the creation to redeem it. There is such a focus on God's present struggle on our behalf, that I wonder whether sufficient ground has been laid for eschatological hope that God will someday be able to redeem us more effectively than she is doing now.

16 Exodus 45: 4-15.

17 Alister McGrath, pp. 284-291. But Marilyn McCord Adams and Kathryn Tanner argue that God acts directly in the world, not through secondary causes. Marilyn McCord Adams, pp 68-69.

18 David Bentley Hart, *The Doors of the Sea*, p. 89.

19 I am flatly disagreeing with D. Z. Phillips here. My fundamental argument with D. Z. Phillips (the reason I side with Marilyn McCord Adams instead) is this: Phillips is right that determining God's connection with evil depends on what we mean by "God." But Phillips' definition, limited by Wittgensteinian linguistic analysis, is of a God who creates the universe but is indifferent to its well-being. Phillips' God sits back waiting to be loved for who he is in his sublime indifference. His is not the Triune God of the Christian tradition, not the God manifest in Jesus, not the Holy Spirit moving with power in our midst. It is not even clear that such a God is lovable.

20 Theologians differ as to the means by which God acts in the world. Some emphasize God's involvement through the action of natural law, which is usually beneficent. Others, such as Thomas Aquinas, have spoken of God's action through "secondary causes." Certainly when people do God's will, acting kindly and justly, we can be such secondary causes. Process theologians emphasize God's influence or persuasion. Pierre Teilhard de Chardin described God as a goal toward which evolutionary processes advance. Alister McGrath, pp. 186-291. Gordon Kaufman adds the more mysterious factor of creative serendipity. Gordon Kaufman, *God in the Face of Mystery* (Cambridge: Harvard University Press, 1993), pp. 264-280.

21 1st Corinthians 13: 12.

22 Adams, p. 147.

23 David Bentley Hart, *The Beauty of the Infinite*, pp. 408-411.

CHAPTER 9

THE SERENE FATHER: THE JOB-DESCRIPTION TRINITY AND SUFFERING

PART 1

"God is our refuge and strength,
    a very present help in time of trouble.
Therefore we will not fear though the earth should change
    though the mountains shake in the heart of the sea;
though its waters roar and foam,
    though the mountains tremble with its tumult. . . .
There is a river whose streams make glad the city of God,
    the holy habitation of the most high.
God is in the midst of her, she shall not be moved . . . .
The Lord of hosts is with us;
    the God of Jacob is our refuge."
      — Psalm 46

WHAT DO WE MEAN BY THE FATHER?

Many people think of the Father as being really God, and of the Son and Holy Spirit as being God's first and second officers. That makes whatever we say about the Father the sum total of what we say about God. Limiting the real God to the Father impoverishes our image of God.[1] In order to allow the metaphor of the Trinity to point toward the rich diversity within God, it is important to remember that the Father is only one of three ways in which God functions. For our purposes, the Father is one of the ways God responds to affliction in the universe.

When we call God "Father," we are saying God is parental toward us. So what kind of a Father is God? The Father's chief attribute is wisdom — vast impenetrable wisdom.[2] It comes of God's unique perspective as the one who was in the beginning, is now, and ever will be — the one who is always and forever everywhere at once. The Father sees things from the viewpoint of eternity, omnipresence (being everywhere), and omniscience (knowing everything). From that perspective, the Father sees how events intensely disturbing to us will nonetheless be redeemed. The Father is the Old Wise One, the Ancient of Days, to whom we can turn when we are in panic, and he can say, "Hush. Hush. Hush. It will be alright."

THE CLASSICAL VIEW: A GOD ABOVE SUFFERING VERSUS THE MODERN VIEW: A SUFFERING GOD

The Early and Medieval Church's way of expressing the Father's balanced, centered wisdom was to say that God is dispassionate, beyond time, beyond change, beyond suffering.[3] Greek philosophers thought feelings were a weakness inconsistent with wise equanimity. Some early theologians argued that when the Son suffered on the cross, the Father suffered with him. The Early Church rejected this argument, calling it a heresy.[4] They insisted that the Father is above such earthly passions.[5] Their point was to portray the Father as strong and stable enough to be able to lift us out of the vicissitudes of life because he was, himself, above them.

In today's culture, we are more apt to construct a sentimental image of God. We want a God who would make a sympathetic guest if he appeared on Oprah. There are serious reasons to object to a God who literally has no feelings, who cannot suffer, who is perpetually anesthetized against personal experience.

The God of Scripture is clearly a passionate God — love, hate, jealously, desperation, worry — clearly a God with a big heart, maybe more heart than head. By his Passion, Jesus reveals God suffering on the Cross. The God of Scripture is no Star Trek Vulcan. Our God is the fountain of the entire panoply of emotions we human beings experience as the flavor of life — joy, sorrow, tenderness, regret, desire, appreciation, even humor. It is incongruous to say that God is love but has no feelings. It is also incongruous to think of God as personal, but without passion.

Consequently, Alfred North Whitehead and the Process Theologians offered us another image of God — "the fellow sufferer who understands." To Whitehead, God is so immanent in creation that God shares all our experience including suffering. He made essentially the same argument, albeit in a more sophisticated way, as the early theologians who claimed the Father suffers in the crucifixion.[6]

Dorothee Soelle criticizes the classical doctrine of divine apathy, because it leads to human apathy in the face of injustice and suffering. We become like the God we worship. If we worship a God who is all-powerful but has no feelings, we strive to become powerful and cold. Soelle sees much in the behavior of contemporary people to suggest that this bad religion is making us worse people, not better. Only a God who cares can teach us to care.[7] The central Christian symbol is the cross, which among other things represents God's compassionate participation in all human pain.[8] How then shall we sort out these diametrically opposed views of God? You have probably already seen this coming — a paradoxical Trinity.

DISPASSION, COMPASSION AND THE TRINITY

The modern picture of a compassionate, suffering God isn't entirely satisfactory. This Suffering God is drowning in the same quicksand we are. Such a suffering God is too weak to be very helpful, or really to be God at all. University of Chicago theologian David Tracy rejects the "fellow sufferer" God image, as did Karl Rahner, who said,

> It does not help me to escape from my mess and mix-up and despair if God is in the same [situation] . . . From the beginning I am locked into its horribleness . . . .[9]

It's good that we are not alone, but we are still sinking. Since the Fellow Sufferer God is in it with us, he can't do us much good.[10] In order to pull us out of the quicksand, we need a God whose feet are planted on firm ground. Our hope depends on the existence of a firm ground somewhere, a reality that isn't subject to the ebb and flow of fortune. When we are drowning, we need a God who can throw us a rope. We need a God who is not swept away by passions as we are. A vulnerable suffering God cannot provide the basis for an unshakeable reality in which we can set our hope.[11]

THE SERENE FATHER: THE JOB-DESCRIPTION TRINITY AND SUFFERING PART 1

The Trinity is a large enough doctrine to encompass both the Serene God Image[12] and the Passionate God Image.[13] Some years ago, there were two popular songs about God. One of them, "From a Distance," described how all human suffering and conflict are reduced to insignificance when placed in a redeeming context by God's "distance." Another, "One of Us," posited the notion of God living our life, sharing our frustration, tedium and anxiety, so that we are fundamentally befriended, not alone. The Trinity invites us to embrace both these ways of thinking about God. In the next chapter, we will find a Passionate God in the Son, the God who is "one of us." In this chapter, we will focus on the other half of the paradox, the Serene Center of reality represented by God the Father who sees all "from a distance," the distance of eternity.

THE SERENE CENTER

The classical description of a dispassionate God is a totally wrong-headed way to think of the Son. Saying that God is dispassionate is a vast over-generalization. It forgets that God, in Jesus, was on the cross. Even calling the Father "dispassionate" is not quite right. The Father is personal and the ideal Father cares for his children. But the Father and the Son relate to us and to our suffering in dramatically different ways. When Early Church teachers called the Father "dispassionate," that word rang well in their ears — not in ours. It portrays the Father too coldly to be a Father we would want. It preserves God's serenity by stripping him of all feeling. We cannot love, worship, or emulate a Star Trek Vulcan God.

We do better to describe the Father as *differentiated*, meaning the Father cares, but calmly, confidently. A differentiated Father *has* feeling without being *overcome* by feeling. The Father remains the still point by having his feelings in balance, remaining perfectly centered because of his unique ability to take the long view of eternity. That long view enables God to allow us our freedom, to allow the creation to run amok for a while. Because of God's unshakable confidence that "all will be well," such a Father cares for us but is not anxious over us. The Father is "the unmoved mover" — "unmoved" in that he is not knocked off balance. Yet God is not the "uncaring mover." God cares for us as a mother cares for her children — but cares with unshaken confidence. While caring, God remains "infinitely at peace."[14] The Father sees our lives from a perspective of

such length and depth and height that our suffering, though never trivial, is surrounded by enough reality to absorb and heal it. The Father God is an infinite spaciousness in which tragedy can be held and contained.[15]

During the same era in which much theology has represented God as a vulnerable "fellow sufferer," countless Westerners have abandoned their faith traditions for Buddhism, Taoism or other belief systems that proclaim a Serene Center such as the Tao, or Sunyata, or Mind representing a vast unity lying deeper than the world's divisions and passions. Such seekers do not want either a tirading patriarch or a martyred suffering Divinity. They are looking for the Serene Center to give them peace. Early Christians knew the Serene Center to be none other than the God "in whom we live and move and have our being."

We deprive Christianity of its greatest source of hope and consolation when we lose our sense of God as an Ocean of Peaceful Wisdom, as the dharma, as the Tao. This larger sense of God was the Greek gift to Christianity. Modern theologians, swayed by excessive biblicism, and giving too little weight to Christian tradition, devalued the Greek contributions to our faith in favor of the Hebrew.[16]

Photo: Stone Mother rock formation, Pyramid Lake, Nevada. / © Copyright Molly Rudd. Used with permission.

Our faith has origins in both Israel and Greece. It limps if they are not both preserved.

A bit of art history suggests something important about the quest for peace and the role of Greek thought in modern religion. Many modern Westerners attracted to Buddhism have never read a sutra, but they are drawn to Buddhism by statues of the serenely meditating Buddha. Early Buddhists, however, did not portray their teacher in art. The serene Buddha statues come from Buddhism's later encounter with Greek culture. The face of the Buddha appears to be modeled on the faces of Greek sculpture from the archaic and classical periods. What many modern Christians seek in Buddhism is actually a lost or suppressed truth in our own faith, and it is found in the Greek contribution to Christianity.

At stake here is our all-important interpretation of God's silence. When we lay our doctrines aside and look honestly at our experience, we must admit that God is often silent. We pray and hear no reply, we plead with God to act, and we see no action. God's silence can be the grave of our faith, or it can be the basis of our faith, depending on how we interpret it. Silence could mean there is no God; or that God does not care about us; or that God exists and cares but is too helpless to even communicate. It is, however, also possible to hear the silence as God's word, a wisdom that transcends discursive speech. God's silence bespeaks stillness, a serenity that is undisturbed — a God who does not sleep but meditates upon creation.[17]

We can hold together in one faith both the changeless God who does not suffer and the "fellow sufferer God" if we just remember two things: (1) Truth claims about God are best stated in paradoxes such as "immanent and transcendent," "three and one," "human and divine." Why not "dispassionate and compassionate," "immutable and responsive?" (2) Anything we say about God has to be offset by an opposite statement. The Trinity allows us to imagine God as possessing attributes that would, for anyone but God, be impossible to combine in one person. So if we are to say God is "dispassionate," we must reinterpret that word to mean something other than "cold." We must think of it instead as meaning infinitely peaceful even while deep caring.

The Early Church was right that there is in God a Serene Center, unmoved, unshaken, eternal, sitting Buddha-like in perfect balance. Given our traditional rejection of the idea that the Father suffers and given that, in the face of the cross, it is rather hard to argue that the

Son does not, we associate this Serene Center with the Father.[18] The Father God is, in T. S. Eliot's words, "The still point of the turning world."

> *At the still point of the turning world...*
> *at the still point, there the dance is...*
> *Except for the point, the still point,*
> *There would be no dance,*
> *And there is only the dance.*

Much of 20th-century's theology completely identifies God with our own vulnerability — it denies the "still point." It wants only the dance; but as Eliot so wisely said, "Except for the still point, there would be no dance."

God comforts us with his own eternity. We may find a Scriptural basis for this idea in Job Chapter 38. I readily grant that Job is subject to a less congenial interpretation.[19] But it is also possible to gather from Job Chapter 38 a beneficent sense of God's differentiated, long-term view. In response to Job's lament arising out of his immediate situation, God answers with his own eternity:

> *Where were you when I laid the foundations of the earth?...*
> *Have you commanded the morning since your days began,*
>   *and caused the dawn to know its place...?*
> *Have you entered into the springs of the sea,*
>   *or walked in the recesses of the deep?*
> *Have the gates of death been revealed to you,*
>   *or have you seen the gates of deep darkness?...*
> *Is it by your wisdom that the hawk soars,*
>   *and spreads his wings toward the south?*
> *Is it at your command that the eagle mounts up*
>   *and makes his nest on high?*

The vastness of God can swallow up our suffering. God's eternity does not spell out meaning, but it sets our sorrows in a larger context. When we are caught up in the immediacy of our own pain, the perspective of eternity can open us to hope and even to the possibility of peace and consolation.

There is a special grace in knowing that the Father God is peaceful and eternal, the Serene Center of Reality. In Shusaku Endo's novel

THE SERENE FATHER: THE JOB-DESCRIPTION TRINITY AND SUFFERING PART 1

Deep River, the Ganges River serves as an image of God. Humanity throngs to the Ganges, all sorts of people with all sorts of suffering. They bathe in the Ganges seeking healing. They pour their grief into the Ganges. Human ashes are poured into the Ganges. The deep and ancient river carries all this with serene dignity.[20] As a hymn puts it: "Time like an ever-rolling stream bears all our cares away."

The ocean is another such image of the Father. The ocean in its stillness by moonlight speaks of eternity. It has a powerful strength and dignity. In his poem "When I Have Fears that I May Cease to Be," John Keats lamented his impending death because it would preclude him from writing all the poems that were in him and because it would separate him from his lover. He says that when these thoughts become too much for him,

". . . then on the shore
Of the wide world I stand alone, and think
Till love and fame to nothingness do sink."

To stand alone on the shore of the wide world is to stand before the eternity of God, and pour our cares into God's eternity until they sink to nothingness. Sometimes our sorrows are so great that we would have to stand on that shore for a very long time indeed. But God gives us forever.

The mystical tradition of Gregory of Nyssa, Dionysius the Areopagite, John Scotus Erigena, the Cloud of Unknowing, Meister Eckhart, and (in our time) Gerald May and Tilden Edwards has connected Christians to the God who is without name or image, who is the unity of all things in eternity. Granted, Christianity also includes "passion mysticism," prayerful union with Christ in the way of the cross, but even that way leads ultimately to the Father who is our peace. The Christian God is more than the tao, not less than the tao. If we are to tell the full truth about God and respond to suffering humanity's need for peace and consolation, Christianity must reclaim its ancient sense of God's Serene Eternity, the same sense that Christian mystics have experienced for two millennia.

Because we believe God suffers — more about that in the next chapter — we believe there is tragedy in God. But, to paraphrase the hermeneutical philosophers, "is it suffering all the way down?" Is God eternally tragic? If God is our destiny as well as our origin, our Alpha and our Omega, then if God is essentially tragic, we are without hope. But we have a brighter view. God is not so simple as the monism of Eastern philosophy, in which union with that ultimate reality is loss of oneself in the Void — but neither is God so broken as the world we now inhabit. God includes a mysterious wisdom but is not devoid of life and passion and longing. The force of life, the passion, are eternally at the core of reality, but embraced within an essential and comprehensive peace.

When Christians speak of union with God, we do not mean non-being, loss of self in the Void, but rather participation in the Trinitarian life. We participate in dynamic on-going life in God energized by longing but sustained by joy. This Trinity, which includes both passion and peace, is our destiny, and we are even now living into our destiny. If we see our destiny as All-Is-One-in-the-Void, a one-note symphony, a one-color painting, a perfect passionless non-dual peace, which dismisses all the ups and downs of mortal life, then we dismiss our experience in this world of chance and change as "only thoughts," as meaningless, as illusion. On the other hand, if we see our destiny as essentially and eternally torn and tragic, then we indulge our feelings as if they were absolute reality deserving to dominate us. But the Trinitarian view of our destiny calls us to live our life, to treasure it and value it. We dare to experience life all the more fully because the fear which holds us back from passion is overcome by the assurance of peace and redemption in our Father God.

CONCLUSION

The Father's eternity and serenity are necessary to our hope. If we are going to offer a God who can save us, we must reclaim that forgotten aspect of God — the Serene Center, the Eye of the Storm. However, the Father's response, standing alone, is infuriatingly aloof. If God remains outside creation, composed and immune to the vicissitudes of transitory life, we feel cut off, utterly removed. Such a God cannot be truly compassionate because he is above the suffering that comes of being trapped in the pain of the present moment. Compassion means, "to suffer with." Such a God is too invulnerable to understand in a personal way what we go though. We can only resent such a God for living imperturbably above while atrocities rage here below.

The Father's serenity is not the whole story, however. In the next chapter, we will see how the Son's compassion plays an equally important role in bringing us through affliction. It is sometimes said that the Book of Job asks a question that is not answered until Jesus. The Father's eternal equanimity (which we see in Job) is an essential part of God's response to suffering; but such equanimity in the face of our affliction is woefully inadequate until it is combined with the compassionate response of the Son.

REFLECTION QUESTIONS

1. When you call God "Father," what do you mean by using that word?

2. Have you ever had the experience of being upset by a situation and going to an older person for advice, support or comfort? What kind of response were you looking for? What kind of response did you receive? What kind of person did you choose?

3. Can you recall a situation in which people you cared for were upset but you felt confident everything would work out? Describe the experience.

4. When the world becomes too much for you, where do you go or what do you do to get some distance? Mountains? Beach? What kind of music do you listen to? How might God be like those places, activities or music?

5. Have you ever had an experience of the Serene Center, perhaps through meditation or prayer? Describe the experience. Did you or do you associate what you encountered as God?

NOTES

1 Treating the Father as the real God, and the Son and Spirit as different ways in which the Father manifests, is essentially the heresy of Sibellian Modalism. Moltmann charges leading Western theologians including Schleiermacher, Barth and even Rahner with being essentially modalist.

2 Alister McGrath, *Christian Theology* (Oxford: Blackwell Publishing, 2001), p. 320. McGrath suggests Old Testament foundations for the doctrine of the Trinity in which the three persons are Wisdom, Word and Spirit.

3 The Early and Medieval theologians used the word "impassible." Alister McGrath, *Christian Theology*, pp. 274-275.

4 It was called *patripassionism*, the suffering of the Father.

5 "This apathy of God has its roots in the thinking of antiquity. This suffering, *pathai*, belongs to the realm of the earthly, in a narrower sense, as suffering and pain, in a wider sense as emotions, drives, passions. God is untouched by all these. Neither the drives nor the compulsions that follow from them can affect him." Dorothee Soelle, *Suffering* (Philadelphia: Fortress Press, 1972), pp. 41-42; See also, Jurgen Moltmann, *The Trinity and the Kingdom*, p. 21, citing J. K. Mozley, *The Impassibility of God: A Survey of Christian Thought* (Cambridge: 1926).

6 Jurgen Moltmann, *The Crucified God* (New York: Harper & Row, 1974). See especially p. 143. Jurgen Moltmann, *The Trinity and the Kingdom* (Minneapolis: Fortress Press, 1993). Moltmann treats the Syrian patripassionists as Docetists who saw the Father as having become the Son and suffered on the cross. His argument is that the Father suffers the loss of his Son and the loss of his fatherhood in handing the Son over to be crucified. Granted, Moltmann's interpretation of the Passion is free of Docetism. But that does not reach the heart of the Church's traditional objection of patripassionism. The problem is that it leaves no room for God's transcendence of suffering. It denies the God who is above the fray and therefore able to lift us out of it in the fullness of time.

7 Dorothee Soelle, *Suffering*, pp. 41-42.

THE SERENE FATHER: THE JOB-DESCRIPTION TRINITY AND SUFFERING PART 1

8 "Moltmann claims support from Abraham Heschel's study of God's passion in the prophets, from kabbalistic Judaism, from early 20th-century Anglican theology, from Miguel Unamuno's classic *The Tragic Sense of Life*; and Nicholas Berdayev's argument that there is 'tragedy' in God." Jurgen Moltmann, *The Trinity and the Kingdom*, pp. 25-47. Philosopher Alvin Plantinga argues that "God's capacity for suffering . . . is proportional to his greatness." Quoted in Adams, *Horrendous Evil and the Love of God*, pp. 23. The belief in God's suffering has been traced back to Luther's "theology of the cross" by Kazho Kitamori. Alister McGrath, *Christian Theology*, p. 278.

9 *Karl Rahner in Dialogue: Conversations and Interviews*, 1965-1982, ed. Paul Imhoff and Hubert Biallowons (New York: Crossroad, 1986), pp. 126-127, quoted in Mark McIntosh, *Mystical Theology* (Oxford: Blackwell Publishers, 1998), p. 153.

10 In fairness, God in process theology is not entirely unable to help. But the metaphorical representation of God as "fellow sufferer" suggests a God who is more of a sympathetic listener than a power for healing and transformation. It is this metaphor to which Rahner, Tracy, and Yale theologian David Kelsey object.

11 "David Bentley Hart regards the rejection of God's "impassibility" or *apatheia*, as "disastrous" because it makes God's state of being dependent on us. That makes God considerably less than the foundation of reality which we have long understood the word "God" to mean, and deprives us of the basis for hope in an unshakeable eternity." David Bentley Hart, *The Doors of the Sea*, pp. 75-77, 81.

12 Rahner, Tracy and Hart.

13 Whitehead, Moltmann and Soelle are theologians of the Passionate God. I am sure Hart would not agree that there is room anywhere in God for suffering. But I stand by my claim that in speaking of God, we can only speak paradoxically, so that both dispassion and compassion can coexist.

14 David Bentley Hart insists that God is not dependent of the vicissitudes of nature and history for anything, so God is, in his words, "infinitely at peace." David Bentley Hart, *The Beauty of the Infinite*, p. 157.

¹⁵ A metaphor for this aspect of God, particularly well attested in Scripture, is the rock.

> "The Rock, his work is perfect...
> A God of faithfulness..." Deuteronomy 32:4
> "There is no rock like our God." I Samuel 2:2
> "Let us make a joyful noise to the rock of our salvation."
> — Psalm 95

The strength and stability of a huge boulder shows us something about God. The rock image in Scripture is by no means intended to suggest God is hard, cold, dissociative, apathetic or removed. It means God is stable, faithful, dependable, "the rock of our salvation," powerful, and unshakable.

¹⁶ With due respect to Robert W. Jensen and Jurgen Moltmann, both great theologians, they too readily treat the Hebrew tradition as authentic and the Greek tradition as inauthentic, notwithstanding the New Testament's being a Greek document. Greek thought was well known to St. Paul, to St. John the Evangelist, and perhaps even to Jesus, who even told an Egyptian story as one of his parables. The rejection of church doctrines developed from Greek philosophy in the patristic era is primarily the work of Adolph Harnack and the "history of dogma" movement. Alister McGrath, *Christian Theology*, pp. 276, 366. While this movement has sometimes been helpful, it has thrown out many a baby with the bath.

¹⁷ "The Indian theologian Raimundo Pannikar interprets God's silence as revealing the core of reality as the serene reconciling of duality which people seek in the Eastern religions." Raimundo Pannikar, *The Silence of God* trans. Robert Barr (New York: Orbis Books, 1989).

¹⁸ As we consider the question of what this view of the Father means for our problem of evil and suffering, it is important to remember several points:
   a. God is not only the Father. This Father is only one aspect of the Triune God.
   b. The Father language is drawn from tradition, but is misleading in that it is gender specific. This is particularly unfortunate in our culture since it may evoke the image of an absentee Father who

is unconcerned with the family because he is pursuing his own interests. That is by no means the point.

c. The point is that God is generative, that God creates reality through a process akin to giving birth, and so Mother would be more apt.

[19] D. Z. Philips and Herman Tennesen regard Job as portraying the divine nature as a contemptible "God of caprice" who offers Job no real redemption at all. D. Z. Phillips, *The Problem of Evil and the Problem of God* (Minneapolis: Fortress Press, 2004), pp. 132-140.

[20] Shusaku Endo, *Deep River.* Trans. Van C. Gessel. New York: New Directions Books. 1994. pp. 194-204.

CHAPTER 10

THE COMPASSIONATE SON: THE JOB-DESCRIPTION TRINITY AND SUFFERING

PART 2

When we think of God the Creator, then we naturally see the rich and powerful of the earth as his closest image. But when we hold steady before us the sight of God the Redeemer redeeming . . . by suffering, then perhaps we must look . . . at the face of that woman with the soup tin in hand and bloated child at side.
— Nicholas Wolterstorff, *Lament for a Son*

Professor Bart Ehrman tells the story of attending a Christmas Eve service in which the intercessor prayed, "You came into our darkness and made a difference. Come into our darkness again." Ehrman says the failure of this prayer is why he cannot be a Christian.

"If God came into our darkness with the advent of the Christ child, bringing salvation to the world, then why is the world in such a state? Why doesn't he enter the darkness again? . . . Why is the darkness so overwhelming? . . . If he came into the darkness and made a difference, why is there still no difference? Why are the sick still wracked with unspeakable pain? Why are babies still born with birth defects? Why are young children, kidnapped, raped, and murdered?" [1]

In contrast to Ehrman's conclusion that if God doesn't "intervene" immediately to take away the pain, God must not exist, let's consider

THE COMPASSIONATE SON: THE JOB-DESCRIPTION TRINITY AND SUFFERING PART 2

David Kelsey's response to the same question in his book *Imagining Redemption*.[2] We previously discussed Kelsey's case study of the little boy who suffers from Gillian-Barre Syndrome, his mother who falls into despair and commits suicide, and his father who struggles as a single dad raising a disabled child. Kelsey puts the question pointedly, "What earthly good does Jesus do in this situation?" But unlike Ehrman, Kelsey comes to a position of faith. Can we? Can we find a way in which God the Son does in fact make a difference? Kesley finds that Jesus makes a profound difference, just not the difference Ehrman expects.

WHAT DO WE MEAN BY 'THE SON'?

When we say "the Son," many people think we simply mean Jesus of Nazareth. They are mostly right. Jesus of Nazareth was the Son in human form. However, John's Gospel, the epistles to the Philippians and the Hebrews, and the creeds are clear that the Son has existed from all eternity. The Son was part of the godhead long before Jesus was born. The Nicene Creed says the Son is "eternally begotten of the Father." The Son has always been part of the Family Trinity. In the Job-Description Trinity, the Son always has always been and always will be a way God connects with creation. Jesus is the fullest occasion of that connection, but God the Son and his involvement with humanity did not begin or end with the earthly life of Jesus of Nazareth.

We encounter the Father and the Son in different ways. The Father appears to us as a vastness, a great distance. The Son is close at hand (immanent), "with us always unto the end of the age." We glimpse the Father aspect of God when something — the desert sky, the mighty river, the mountain, the ocean — evokes the perspective of eternity. There is a spiritual truth in the large view, the panoramic scope of infinity, the "God's eye" view in which we and all around us become small. But there is also a truth in the direct experience of this moment — now, now and now.

The Son appears to us as the present moment. Russian poet and novelist Boris Pasternak said, ". . . [T]he instant (far more than hours and ages) is eternity's rival."[3] The 17th-century Jesuit Jean-Pierre de Causade wrote of "the sacrament of the Present Moment." Buddhist writers including Thich Nhat Hahn construct an entire spirituality out of attention to this instant. "Be here now," Ram Dass said. It is appropriate and no coincidence that Alfred North Whitehead, who gave us the God image of the "fellow sufferer who understands," described reality as consisting of discrete present moments. We find the Father in the big picture; we find the Son close at hand right now. This may be St. Mark's point in beginning so many sentences about Jesus with the word, "immediately."

HOW THE SON RESPONDS TO SUFFERING

Jesus reveals how the Son responds to our suffering. In the Gospels, we see Jesus searching and longing just as we do — going to John for Baptism, seeking his mission in the desert, trying unsuccessfully to explain himself in his hometown, exhausted and retiring for prayer, weeping over the fate of Jerusalem, seeking deliverance in Gethsemane. All the while, he lives among us as one of us, he teaches, he heals, he suffers and dies. Then he is resurrected and ascends to glory. In all of this, the Son participates in and responds to our human situation. Too often theologians focus exclusively on the crucifixion of Our Lord as his response to suffering. The crucifixion is, no doubt, at the heart of the story, but it is not the whole story. If we are to have a comprehensive picture of how the Son meets us in our times of trial, we must consider the entire Jesus story from birth through the Ascension.

The historical story of Jesus is part of the Son's response to suffering. However, it is more than that. The Jesus story reveals how the Eternal Son always responds. The Son suffers with us. The Son is the Compassion of God, feeling what we feel every bit as much as we do.[4] Still we must ask what difference the Son's response makes.[5] There are two basic kinds of response to the question of "what earthly good" does the Son do for us in our suffering?[6] One is substitutionary. Jesus suffers in our stead. The other is compassionate. Jesus suffers at our side.

SUFFERING IN OUR STEAD

The substitutionary theory holds that Jesus suffers on our behalf so we will not have to bear that pain. The underlying premise is that our afflictions are punishments for our sins. Jesus helps by taking some of the punishment for us. We deserve far more affliction than we actually suffer. We have actually gotten out of much of our well-deserved torment, because Jesus suffered such a large share of our penalty on the cross. However, we still have to pay for the excess over and above what Jesus has suffered.[7] The theory may be extended to the eternal Son by saying he still suffers when we sin and thereby continues to bear the brunt of our guilt.

    This way of thinking is profoundly unsatisfactory. We have already observed that suffering falls far too randomly to be understood as punishment for sin. Jesus himself did not accept this notion. Portraying God as the punisher from above may instill "fear of the Lord" but not devotion to the Lord. That is just the beginning of what's wrong with the substitutionary model. According to this way of thinking, Christ has proven only somewhat effectual. As for the suffering we still endure, it is cold comfort to be told we deserve worse. Moreover, this account utterly disregards Jesus' teaching and healing ministries as signs of the Son's response to our affliction. In fact, it sides with the Pharisees who opposed Jesus' healing ministry because it undermined the just retribution of God. This model has no role for the Resurrection in addressing our affliction. Finally, this dark doctrine portrays God as an abusive father torturing and murdering his Son. In *Naked Before God*, Bill and Martha Williams offer a compelling rebuttal to such a brutal theology.

One Sunday Martha asked her [Sunday school] kids what they thought about God... "Well, she said... "Is he good or bad or what?" One of them — we'll call him Timothy — looked at her and said... "Well,... God killed his Son."

Shut your ears Timothy! You're listening too well... You just hold on to the notion that God is good, not evil, and that loving you doesn't mean he wants to kill you. If you let that filth in, you'll spend your life trying to scrape it off. When they start to bleat that poison in the big room just plug your ears and chant with me: God is good. God is good. God is good. That will be our measuring stick, you and me. If anything doesn't measure up to that, you'll know it's broken... Don't believe that God is the Devil no matter what your church says. God is good...[8]

    Bart Ehrman looks at the Christ-event, the Incarnation, and sees that it has not "made a difference." If the "difference" he is looking for is the cessation of suffering, he is dead right. It has not made that difference, but we must look deeper to see if it may have made another kind of difference.

SUFFERING AT OUR SIDE

There is a better way to understand how the Son helps us. In the Cross, God the Son identifies with our suffering — compassionately, not manipulatively. God is so present with the hungry that his stomach cramps. God is so present with the lonely that his throat constricts and cannot call out for comfort. God is so present with the grief-stricken that he cannot move. But God does not suffer at our hands to make us feel guilty. Rather God suffers with us to make us feel loved. God's suffering is compassionate, not manipulative.[9]

When we become like this kind of God, we relate to suffering, our own and that of others, in a different way. We acknowledge our own pain, then notice that we aren't the only ones who feel this way. We take off the blinders and dare to look at the suffering of others — the suffering of abject poverty in Haiti and Zimbabwe, the suffering of shame and remorse in the people right next to us. When we take off the blinders, we see right off that all forms of suffering are essentially the same. Life hurts. We all hurt. We all have to go to the cross.

But we do not go to the cross without hope if we go to the cross together with Christ and with each other. When we bleed together, that's Communion. And Communion is the Divine Nature. That's what the Trinity signifies. Compassion connects us to eternity and the soul of eternity extends beyond suffering. The soul of eternity is the Father's peace and wisdom and serenity. And the heart of eternity is the exuberant joy that created the universe and fills it with life and beauty. That's where compassion leads.

This part of the divine response to suffering is often trivialized. It is apt to be misconstrued as nothing more than saying, "Jesus understands what we are going through." Mere understanding is a long way from real redemption. Understanding is a good thing to have from one's friends and family, but one might hope for more from God. As Kelsey says, "Redemption is something beyond giving comfort."[10] When one has just been diagnosed with a life-threatening cancer, the attention of one's friend is welcome, but one is more interested in the help of a first-rate oncologist. The redemption we read about in the New Testament is more substantive than the promise of a fellow sufferer to "be there for us." The New Testament repeatedly affirms that our heartaches not only share in the suffering of Christ and take us to the same cross, but also will lead us to the same comfort, healing, and resurrection. 1st Corinthians 1:15; Philippians 3: 10-11; 1st Peter 4: 12-13. Ultimately, these are promises for eter-

THE COMPASSIONATE SON: THE JOB-DESCRIPTION TRINITY AND SUFFERING PART 2

nity. But is there a way in which the Son's joining us in the human predicament changes the situation now? Is there resurrection for us now because the Son is in this with us? There are four helpful ways to think of how the Son's compassion represented by the cross can redeem our pain.

Liberating Our Identity from Suffering

Kelsey offers a helpful variation on the "fellow sufferer" model when he turns to the question of what makes one's life worth living. We are apt to justify our lives by identifying with our role as victim or as one who has survived something captivatingly horrific. Such identifications, however, bind us to the worst parts of our past and cut us off from joy and from the unfolding, vital, dynamic future. This is decidedly a common response to suffering, and it is psychologically crippling and spiritually atrophying.[11]

Kelsey proposes a healthier kind of redemption: Jesus' crucifixion reveals God's love for us. The Son does not have to suffer. Nothing

Photo: A grief stricken American infantryman whose buddy has been killed in action is comforted by another soldier. / Wikimedia Commons.

compels him to go to the cross. Rather, the Son chooses to join us in our pain. Jesus shows us a God who values us enough to join us in our suffering instead of sitting blissfully serene in Paradise. If we can find our identity in being loved this much by God instead of by attaching our identity to our defining tragedy, then we are set free from the tragedy's power to define us.[12]

Evoking Love

Redemption achieved by the compassionate suffering of the Son is, however, more comprehensive than the liberation of our identities from tragedy. In the 11th century, Peter Abelard argued that the suffering and death of Christ saves us by revealing God's love, and inspiring us to love God in return. This stirring up of our love for God sets us free from bondage to sin and self. Abelard gave us a medieval precursor of the fellow sufferer who understands. He also gave us a psychologically credible foundation for the notion that suffering can be spiritually helpful.[13]

The question remains what difference loving God makes when we are suffering. The answer is neither simple nor rational in a linear sense. But experience validates it. Suffering can make us turn inward upon ourselves. We fixate on our pain. The result is embittering and atrophying. We not only suffer because of what has happened to us. We compound the pain by suffering because we suffer. So many of the books on the problem of evil are exercises in precisely this compounding of affliction. But if we turn our attention and energy outward — to love another person, or to serve a higher cause — the suffering, though not diminished, can be borne. This is what Victor Frankl saw in the concentration camps. Love and meaning can often get us through what otherwise could not be endured. If we turn our energy all the way outward, to love Eternity itself, Reality itself, to love God, that love is salvific.

Transforming Suffering into a Place We Meet God

Healing us by evoking love in us is decidedly part of what the Son can do. But that healing depends on our response. It depends on our belief in God's love. Does redemption depend entirely on our subjective understanding and belief? Is there more going on in the Son's response to human affliction than a shift in our psychology, something objective, not dependent on whether people "get it?"[14] The answer is "yes." God's joining us in our pain is an act of love, and that makes a real difference, whether we "get it" or not. Of course, if we acknowledge and accept grace, we experience the blessing all the more, but the blessing is there by God's act. It doesn't depend on our understanding it.

Paul wrote that something had actually happened in the death and resurrection of Christ, that the world had been objectively changed. In the 4th century, St. Athanasius, one of the most influential people in shaping the Christian understanding of God, Jesus and salvation, said salvation turned on the notion that when God "assumed" something — took it on, made it part of the divine experience — whatever had been assumed was redeemed. Kathryn Tanner applies that idea to Jesus' experience of human suffering. She writes:

The humanity assumed by the Word suffers from the effects of sin . . . tempted, anxious before death, surrounded by sufferings of all kinds, in social conditions of exclusion and political conflict. The Word's assuming or bearing of all this means a fight with it . . .[15]

Tanner's argument is grounded in the mystical apprehension that when God walks a path, the path is changed. Such an argument is difficult to articulate; but it is intuitively compelling. If Christ has suffered as we suffer, that must make a difference. But *what difference* does it make?

Marilyn McCord Adams contends that our ultimate redemption from suffering is found in our relationship with God whose Goodness and Beauty vastly exceed all the ills of the created order. By joining in the experience of suffering, God makes suffering a common ground, an occasion to establish the human-divine relationship that will ultimately redeem us and bring us to joy. Adams does not offer this argument as a cause of or justification for suffering. Rather she is saying this is how God turns otherwise meaningless suffering into something of positive value.

Divine identification with human participation in horrors confers a positive aspect on such experiences by integrating them into the participant's relationship with God.[16]

Our joining with God in suffering does not, however, mean we stay in suffering in order to stay with God. We pass through suffering together on the way to joy. Paul prayed to share the suffering of

Christ *in order that he might share the resurrection of Christ.* Tanner insists that Christ did not suffer in order to enshrine suffering, but to overcome it. Jesus assumed affliction, taking on human pain and vulnerability, all the way into a disgraceful death, and then overcame that affliction in the resurrection and ascension. That has made a basic difference in the order of things. Suffering and death still happen, but they do not get the final word. This divine action permeates all situations with hope. "Blessed be the God and Father of our Lord Jesus Christ for by his great mercy we have been born anew to a living hope through the resurrection of Jesus Christ from the dead."[17]

Tanner's reminder that Christ suffers in order to overcome suffering, not abide in it, is particularly important when we think of the Eternal Son always sharing our pain. If we understand the Son's only response to be suffering alongside us, then we deify suffering, get stuck in it, and fail to avail ourselves of the power to rise up and live. The Holy Spirit infuses that power, and our consideration here of most of this aspect of the divine response to suffering will be in the next chapter. However, so that we do not misunderstand the value of Christ's compassion, we need to clarify the meaning of the cross for our lives. If we are to think of the cross as Christ eternally sharing our sorrow, we must match that image with the Resurrection as Christ eternally rising up from sorrow so that we may rise with him. Veneration of the crucifix, of Christ on the cross, must not obscure celebration of resurrection as Christ's power of life continuing to happen for us now.

We may well ask why we have to meet God in suffering. Can we not, yea do we not, encounter God in joy? Don't we see a beautiful day and thank God for it? When we are deeply loved by another person, don't we thank God for him or her? We do meet God in the good times. But the good times don't need an independent justification. They are just plain good. What if God chose to meet us in the good times and leave us alone in the bad ones? Then the bad ones would be meaningless. There would be nothing to redeem them. But if God chooses to stay with us, for better or worse, in sickness and in health, then we meet God in a special way, a better way, than if God were a fair weather friend.

This assumption theory of redemption is a narrative of hope, of "the Word becoming flesh" to endure suffering, and eventually to triumph over death itself through the resurrection. Jesus' life of healing, reconciling and teaching is a sign of how the Son is always present, working for the good in our human situation. His death and resurrection reveal how the eternally faithful God will make all well in the fullness of time.[18]

Suffering to Become Our Mediator

Hebrews offers a further interpretation of our salvation story in which the Ascension is as vital a part of our salvation as the Incarnation, the Crucifixion, or the Resurrection. Hebrews says we need a bridge between mortal, frail, fallible humanity and God — a personal bridge, an intermediary, to plead our case, to tell the Infinite what it is like to be finite, to tell the Perfect what it is like to be fallible, to tell the Serene Center of the Reality how it feels to be afraid. Such a bridge must be at home both in heaven and on earth. He must be truly God and truly human.[19]

In Jesus, God the Son took on flesh lived a human life and died an all too human death. Hebrews tells us that the Son is God from all eternity, before all time. He then took human form. He had to live and suffer his way into becoming fully human so he could serve as the bridge. We need someone to tell the Serene Center what we are experiencing. And we need someone to assure us that the Serene Center cares for us. Jesus forges the link between human passion and divine serenity. A helpful metaphor might be to think of the Father and Son as connected by the Spirit as the ocean is connected to the moon by gravity. The movement of the Son, the suffering of the Son with us, effects a merciful tide in the oceanic Father.[20]

CONCLUSION

Our faith is that God the Son has come into our darkness and he comes into it over and over again. He does make a difference. It may not be the difference we want. It is not what Ehrman means by a difference. But it is the difference between suffering without meaning in a cold indifferent universe (such as Camus paints in *The Stranger*) versus suffering with God in a way that connects us to love. It is the difference between hope and despair.

We have seen God responding to our suffering now in two ways — with wise equanimity and with compassion. These responses help more than words can say — but they are not enough. When we have been laid low, we need to be raised up. That brings us to the work of the Holy Spirit.

REFLECTION QUESTIONS

1. What value does the suffering of Jesus on the cross have for you in your life? Is it suffering in your stead or suffering at your side?

2. Have you known anyone who was stuck in identifying with his or her suffering? How did that identification seem to affect his or her life?

3. Have you had the experience of someone voluntarily sharing a hardship with you? How did it make you feel abut them? Did your feeling for them change your experience of suffering?

4. In what situations do you believe you can meet God?

5. Have you ever been lifted out of suffering by an experience of joy or beauty? Describe the experience.

6. In your prayer, have you thought of Christ as a mediator? How might you ask him to help?

NOTES

[1] Bart Ehrman, God's Problem: How *The Bible Fails to Answer Our Most Important Question — Why We Suffer* (New York: Harper Collins, 2008), p. 5.

[2] David Kelsey, *Imagining Redemption* (Louisville: Westminster John Knox Press, 2005).

[3] Letter to Marina Tsveteyeva, July 1, 1926 in *Letters, Summer 1926*, ed. Yevgeny Pasternak, Yelena Pasternak, Konstantin M. Azadovsky. trans. Margaret Wettlin, Walter Arndt, Jamey Gambrell (New York: The New York Review of Books, 2001), p. 208.

[4] There is the Protestant emphasis that Christ's sacrifice was made *once*; it does not have to be repeated. That teaching, derived from the Book

of Hebrews, is not meant to deny that Christ compassionately shares our pain. It is meant to reject a medieval understanding of the Mass. The underlying assumption of that medieval idea, derived from St. Anselm's doctrine of the atonement, was that Christ's suffering was a substitution, Christ suffering to pay the penalty for our sins. Baptism served to accept the benefit of that sacrifice. But what about the sins we commit after being baptized? Some medieval Christians believed Christ had to be sacrificed anew in each mass to propitiate God to forgive our more recent transgressions. The idea that there was only one sacrifice of substitution was meant to correct that distortion of what the celebration of Holy Communion truly is, an encounter with God in love. The whole notion of a sacrifice of substitution is questionable anyway, but the idea that it has to be carried out over and over is even worse. The "one sacrifice" doctrine addresses that point. It has nothing to do with understanding the cross as a sign of Christ's constant compassion, of his being with us to the ends of the age, including in our suffering.

5   There is a huge part of this question I will not attempt to address here. Theologians customarily treat it separately, and it is a book unto itself. That is the question of how the Son's response to our human situation redeems the evil we ourselves commit. Answers to that question are called Doctrines of Atonement. I will limit this book to the question of how the Son's response may be helpful for the evil we suffer at the hands of others or at the hands of nature.

6   Of course, the question of what the Son does for us is larger than the question of what good he does for us in our suffering. The matter of atonement for sin is another question, perhaps not unrelated, but certainly not the same. Our focus here is on suffering.

7   This viewpoint was not widely held in Christianity for the first 1,000 years of our history. But, beginning with St. Anselm (10th century), and then even more so after John Calvin (16th century) the most common understanding of Jesus' suffering is that he is taking the beating which the Father would otherwise be compelled by his sense of justice to administer to us. Theologians call this "penal substitution" or "the substitutionary atonement" doctrine.

8   Bill Williams and Martha Williams, *Naked Before God* (Harrisburg: Morehouse Publishing, 1998), pp. 240-241. See also Gray Temple,

The Molten Soul (New York: Church Publishing, Inc., 2000) in which Fr. Temple argues that this theory of the atonement is destructive to a vital spiritual life and leads to rigidity and judgmental attitudes.

[9] C. E. Rolt and Charles Hartshorne portray God's suffering love as a compassionate gesture of solidarity with people, and thus a gesture toward personal relationship. Adams, pp. 70-71, 159 -161.

[10] David Kelsey, pp. 54-55.

[11] See also Gerald May, at 98-201 in which Dr. May describes our addictions to self-representations or ways of thinking of ourselves.

[12] David Kelsey, pp. 55-59.

[13] We must be careful here not to fall into the misunderstanding that arises when people mix Christ's compassion up with the notion that Christ continues to suffer affliction whenever we commit sin and because we commit sin. The cross is meant to communicate love, not instill guilt. This is not a matter of our afflicting Christ but of Christ sharing our affliction. Love liberates. Guilt enslaves.

[14] Kelsey intends his redemption model to be objective as well as subjective.

[15] Kathryn Tanner, *Jesus, Humanity, and Trinity*. (Minneapolis: Fortress Press, 2001), pp. 27-28.

[16] Adams, pp. 166-167.

[17] 1 Peter 1:3

[18] This approach should not be allowed to detract from the vital fact of the historical event of Jesus. To say all too abstractly that the Son is always with us is not deeply helpful unless that abstraction is enfleshed in the story of Jesus. Only when it really happens in the particular event can we take it seriously as a general principle.

[19] This model of redemption runs contrary to Robert W. Jensen's understanding. He insists at p. 83 that "Since relation to us, as the Father

of our Lord, is internal to God's being, there is no need for bridge-beings between God and us." Part of Jensen's objection to a bridge concept of Christ is that it suggests another metaphor, a more problematic one, a "ladder of divinity" in which the Trinity is made up of successively more divine beings leading from humanity to God. p. 90. The bridge or mediation model of Hebrews is no such ladder of divinity. The fully divine Logos becomes fully human through living a human life in order that he may act as our mediator.

However, Jensen's objection to a bridge between humanity and God goes deeper. It rests in his repudiation of Greek notions of eternity. Jensen sees God in Hebrew terms. He is concerned to avoid Arius' idea that God must be entirely uninvolved with time in order to save us from time. p. 81. Jensen notes critically, "(T)he religion of late antiquity was a frenzied search for mediators, for beings of a third ontological kind between time and Timelessness, to bridge the gap." p. 61. Arius was wrong in trying to keep all of God uncontaminated by time. But the Greek longing to transcend time is deeply entrenched in Christian tradition. In the model of the Trinity proposed in this book, the Father metaphor refers to the aspect of God which manifests as eternity and is untouched by time so that he is able to offer hope to us " . . . who are wearied by that changes and the chances of this life that we may rest in thy eternal changelessness." (*The Book of Common Prayer*). The Son, however, is God immanent in time, fully involved and faithfully present with us through "the changes and the chances of this life." Christianity is a "religion (born in) late antiquity" and Christ does in fact mediate "between time and Timelessness, to bridge the gap."

[20] "In union with God, in being brought near to God, all the trials and sorrows of life — suffering, loss, moral failing, the oppressive stunting of opportunities and vitality, grief, worry, tribulation, and strife — are purified, remedied, and reworked through the gifts of God's grace." Kathryn Tanner, p. 2.

CHAPTER 11

THE REVITALIZING SPIRIT: THE JOB-DESCRIPTION TRINITY AND SUFFERING

PART 3

Holy Spirit,
giving life to all life,
moving all creatures,
root of all things,
washing them clean,
wiping out their mistakes,
healing their wounds,
you are our true life,
luminous, wonderful,
awakening the heart
from its ancient sleep.
— Hildegard of Bingen

And we know when Moses was told
    in the way he was told,
"Take off your shoes!" He grew pale from that simple
reminder of the fire in the dusty earth...
Like the moment you too saw for the first time,
    your own house turned to ashes.
Everything consumed so the road could open again.
Your entire presence in your eyes
    and the world turning slowly
into a single branch of flame.
— David Whyte, "Fire in the Earth" from *Fire in the Earth*

THE REVITALIZING SPIRIT: THE JOB-DESCRIPTION TRINITY AND SUFFERING PART 3

We have seen that the Father's wise serenity can be our eye in the hurricane. We have seen that the Son's compassion consoles us and gives meaning to suffering that might otherwise be for nothing. But there is more yet to God's redemption; it is the reviving, empowering, restorative action of the Holy Spirit. In this chapter we will consider how the Spirit raises us up from desolation and despair.

WHAT DO WE MEAN BY 'THE HOLY SPIRIT?'

The Greek word for "spirit" is *pneuma*, which means breath or wind. "The wind (*pneuma*) blows where it wills and you hear the sound of it, but you do not know whence it comes or whither it goes."[1] We know the Holy Spirit through its actions in our midst. It blows through us like a Chinook wind through a western canyon, speaking with mysterious voices.[2] It will be nigh unto impossible to see how the Spirit responds to our affliction unless we liberate our understanding from a widely held way of thinking of the Spirit, a way too small for our purposes.

Many people today confuse the Holy Spirit with religious emotions, especially ecstasy. I am not denigrating religious emotions; however, there is a serious problem with interpreting any feeling as being the Holy Spirit. One of the very fathers of emotionally charged religion in America, the 18th-century evangelist Jonathan Edwards, came to a sober appreciation of the place of feeling in faith. On one hand he said, "True religion consists in great part in holy affections [feelings]." But that does not make our feelings, even our holy feelings, the same as the Holy Spirit, which is God.[3] Our feelings are too flimsy, too flighty, and too easily manipulated to be equated with the eternally faithful God. When our feelings are strong and good, they may be our response to the Holy Spirit, but they are not the Holy Spirit. It is especially important for suffering people to know the Spirit is more than their feelings. Being depressed or overwrought with grief is a long way from religious ecstasy — but that doesn't mean the Holy Spirit is not present in those situations actively working to heal and redeem.[4]

The Spirit is the divine force that gives and restores life. At the Council of Constantinople in 381 C. E., the Church named the Spirit "the Lord, the Giver of Life."[5] The Nicene Creed affirms the Spirit's presence in the life-giving sacraments and concludes with our hope for resurrection, which is also the action of the Spirit. God gave Adam life by breathing into his nostrils God's own *ruach*/breath/spirit. Duke theologian Geoffrey Wainwright finds three roles of the Spirit in the Hebrew Scriptures. The Spirit issues from God first, to create; second, to give life; and third, to empower prophets, judges, kings, and warriors.[6]

St. Paul teaches that the Spirit dwells in us, but we also dwell in the Spirit.[7] We experience the Spirit inwardly, but the Spirit is not limited to our interiority. The Spirit fills us just as breath fills our lungs and infuses our blood with oxygen, but the air we breathe extends around the world and far into the sky. The Spirit is vastly larger than we are. It permeates us but we cannot contain it.

All of this is just a preliminary idea of who the Spirit is. We really get to know the Holy Spirit by seeing what the Spirit does — particularly how the Spirit responds to human suffering.

THE SPIRIT REVITALIZES AND EMPOWERS US

Sometimes I feel discouraged and like my life's in vain.
But then the Holy Spirit revives my soul again.
    — Hymnal 1982, "There is a Balm in Gilead"

When Jesus lay dead in the tomb, the Spirit breathed life back into him. Just so, the Spirit restores our life when we are in death. When we are dead, physically, spiritually, morally or emotionally, the Spirit breathes life back into us. The Spirit is the force that raises us from death.[8] When we go to the cross of our own affliction, the Son goes with us. Because he has gone with us, the Spirit, who raised Jesus, raises us too. This is the force Paul calls the "Spirit of Life" and the Creed calls "the Lord, the Giver of Life."[9] The afflicted are restored by this animating, vivifying energy of God stirring within our souls and all around us.

Life is often more than we can bear. And yet, to our utter amazement, people do rise from their ashes and walk on, sometimes heroically, wisely, compassionately — occasionally, even joyfully. When this happens, we know we are witnessing a miracle and a mystery. Human beings are not this resilient. No one could be. And yet, it happens.

Ultimately, our hope lies in the final resurrection[10] in which all the broken, bruised, crushed and disheartened will be healed, made

THE REVITALIZING SPIRIT: THE JOB-DESCRIPTION TRINITY AND SUFFERING PART 3

whole, and glorified. Every tear will be wiped away from every eye. All will be forgiven, restored and resolved. But we don't have to wait that long to see the work of the Spirit. Those who suffer know full well we cannot wait that long. Resurrection happens — and it must happen if we are to have hope to carry us forward — now, in the midst of this mortal life, when the sufferer whose life seems to be over gets up and takes the next step, draws the next breath. This is the action of the Holy Spirit, the divine breath, the wind at our backs, carrying us forward. The Holy Spirit dwells within us, but the Spirit is bigger than we are. It would have to be for the miracles it must perform.

Sometimes when disaster or disappointment strikes, we say, "it knocked the wind out of my sails." A loss, a discouragement can sap our energy to live. The French term is *envie de continuer* — the will to go on. When we lose that will, it is like losing God's spirit. That is why the psalmist prayed in Psalm 51, "Take not your holy spirit from me . . . Sustain me with your bountiful spirit." Again think of lifeless Adam in creation or lifeless Jesus in the tomb vivified by God's breath of life blown into their bodies.

In Ezekiel 37, the prophet surveys the Valley of Dry Bones. The bones represent the despairing people of Israel in exile in Babylon. Israel says, "Our bones are dried up and our hope is lost." But the Lord says to the hopeless, forsaken exiles, taken from their homeland and enslaved, "I will put my Spirit in you, and you shall live."

Photo: Wind in the sails / © Copyright Byrne Chapman. Used with permission.

Both Paul and Ezekiel portray the Spirit as breathing life and hope back into us. St. John gives us a different figure of speech. In John's account of Jesus' farewell discourse, Our Lord says,

> *I will pray to the Father, and he will give you another Paraklete [variously translated as Comforter, "Advocate or "Counselor"] to be with you forever, even the Spirit of Truth.*[11]

William Temple emphasized that "Paraklete" means a strengthener more than a consoler.[12] John Macquarrie says the work of the Holy Spirit in humankind is to "enlighten and strengthen" us.[13] The Spirit empowers us to stand up on our feet and live.

This Spirit gives us life when we are in death, empowers us to do what must be done. Just as the Spirit raised up and sustained the prophets, judges, kings and warriors of Israel, the Spirit inspires us to do more than our own strength could accomplish. In the face of affliction, we need power. Sometimes it is the power to show up for another round of chemotherapy; sometimes, it is the power to fight an injustice; sometimes it is the power to resist an addictive impulse. We often don't have that power within ourselves. But the Holy Spirit has deep wells of power available to strengthen us.

The Spirit revives our souls, imbuing us with inner strength. But remember, the Spirit is more than what happens inside us. The Spirit is the life force of all creation, not limited by our subjectivity, not homebound in our interiority. Some theologians seem reluctant to acknowledge the place of gracious serendipity in our lives. Perhaps it comes too close to religious naiveté and superstition for their liking. However, even the generally skeptical and rationalist theologian Gordon Kaufman acknowledges creative serendipity as God's hand in the on-going development of the cosmos and in human history.[14] Gracious serendipity happens in our individual lives too. Someone says the right word. An unexpected opportunity comes along. The right book falls into our hands when we weren't looking for it. Healing happens by ordinary or extraordinary means. "The wind blows where it wills . . ."

This is not to say the Spirit is orchestrating everything that happens; but the Spirit is present in every situation, not controlling it, but calling it, inviting it, luring it toward mercy, justice, and reconciliation. How the Spirit acts in gracious serendipity is utterly beyond explanation. But, God as my witness, it does happen. The Spirit acts

LIVING BEYOND SELF

Earlier, I told the story of a woman who lost her daughter in the crash of TWA Flight 800. She asked me "why" and I had no answer. She later found an answer — not to the question "why" but to the more important question of "how then shall we live"? Another woman in our congregation, a lonely person with no family, was dying of renal failure. Someone had to care for her. So the grieving mother got up from her grief and took food to the dying woman. She joined with others in the congregation to give the care a family might have given if there had been one. The mother says today that the dying woman saved her life. How? By needing her.

When the Spirit raises us from despair, it does not just restore us to our old life. We do not just carry on as before. Life in the Spirit is new life with a new agenda. When the Spirit of God fell upon prophets or kings, it was not just to cheer them up, but also to empower them for a mission of service to others. Paul is emphatic in I Corinthians 12 and 13 that spiritual gifts aren't for the benefit of individuals. Life in the Spirit means life for others. Jesus, applying the words of Second Isaiah to himself, said:

The Spirit of the Lord is upon me
　　because he has anointed me
to preach good news to the poor . . .
to proclaim release to the captives
　　and recovery of sight to the blind
to set at liberty those who are oppressed
and to proclaim the acceptable year of the Lord.[15]

The Spirit draws us outside ourselves into concern for and service to others, particularly the afflicted. Christians and non-Christians alike equate spirituality too much with practicing the right meditations or holding the right beliefs so we can maintain a pleasant mood. But that isn't how the Holy Spirit works. Spirit-filled persons are not that interested in their own mood. They are thinking about "the poor, the blind, and the oppressed."[16]

The Spirit calls and empowers people to help those who are poor, blind, oppressed, held captive or subject to any form of affliction. The Spirit serves the suffering through the hands of flesh-and-blood human servants. And the Spirit lifts us out of our suffering by transforming us into servants.

When we are wounded, it is natural to become focused on our own pain and loss. It is natural for our attention to turn inward. It is even natural to identify with our status as an innocent victim. Natural as these responses are in the immediate aftermath of a loss, they are the very responses that, over time, cripple us and prevent us from moving on to experience new life. Liberation from this disabling identification is part and parcel of restoring our wholeness.[17] The Spirit sets us free from obsessive thinking, from the power of systems, from old patterns of feeling and acting that keep us trapped in lives less than God wants for us. The Spirit liberates us by converting our self-focus to service. Our own pain can become the raw material of compassion for others. That transformation is a healing in itself and it opens our hearts to further healing over time. The Prayer of St. Francis says, "It is in giving that we receive; it is in forgiving that we are forgiven . . ." Just so, it is in healing others that we ourselves are healed.

Life in the Spirit is life for others. Life lived for self is the spiritual death from which the Spirit raises us. When Paul contrasts flesh and Spirit, he is not contrasting bodily instincts with intellectual or ascetic values. He uses flesh as a metaphor of egocentricity. Some modern translations bypass the metaphor by translating *sarx* (literally, flesh) as self-indulgence. Paul says the works of the flesh or self-indulgence are fornication, impurity, licentiousness, idolatry, sorcery, enmity, strife, jealousy, anger, selfishness, dissension, partisanship, envy . . . . But the fruit of the Spirit is love, joy, peace, patience, kindness, goodness, faithfulness, gentleness, self-control."[18] The Spirit sets us free from self-obsession and opens our hearts to care for others through active service.[19]

CONNECTING THE DISCONNECTED

Severe suffering breaks our connection with reality at a fundamental level. We may deny the reality of our loss; or we may be swallowed up by it so that we cannot appreciate what remains or take in new life as it unfolds. Either way, we are cut off. The Spirit reconnects us. Rowan Williams says, "the Spirit connects us to reality in a way that bridge[s] . . . the gulf between suffering and hope . . . confronting suffering without illusion but also without despair."[20] It does not lift us out of our experience. It directly connects us with the reality at hand, which may actually lift us out of our subjectivity, our personal myths and habitual ways of interpreting things. The Spirit links us to the reality of our pain, but also to the reality of our hope. It connects us to the present moment, but it also connects us to eternity.[21]

The ultimate action of the Holy Spirit is to connect us with God. The Spirit draws us into the Trinity, into the swirling vortex of Trinitarian Love. The Spirit's power to reconnect us to the realities at hand is part and parcel of the Spirit's role in the inner life of God. There is a dynamic tension between the Father and the Son — the Father's "still point" serenity and the Son's passion. The tension between them is creative and alive. That tension vibrates like the rhythm of African drums. And in that tension is the dance. The Holy Spirit is the dance. We might think of the Job-Description Trinity, in this context, as the Dancer (the Son), the Still Point (the Father), and the Dance (the Spirit).

When the Spirit gives us direct awareness of the Present Moment in which the Son manifests, and of Eternity in which the Father manifests, and when the Spirit empowers us to live into the dynamic tension of those two poles, we have joined the dance. We are living in the Spirit and participating in God. We need as much consolation and encouragement as we can get in this life. But ultimately we need more. We need redemption. We need to reach a destination that justifies the journey, "the bitter road we've trod." That redemption is our union with God in the cosmic dance. Another way to express this redeeming action of the Spirit is Paul's image of adoption:

All who are led by the Spirit are sons of God . . .
When we cry "Abba! Father!" it is the Spirit himself
bearing witness with our spirit that we are children
of God." [22]

When we are raised from our spiritual death by the same Spirit that raised Christ, drawn by the Spirit beyond our self-focus, and empowered by that Spirit to serve others, to "proclaim good news to the poor and release to the captives . . . ," then we stand as brothers of Christ and children of the Father. The Spirit's response to affliction is not a sedative, not a soothing reassurance, but a profoundly new life. As David Whyte says:

> Like the moment you too saw for the first time,
>   your own house turned to ashes.
> Everything consumed so the road could open again.
>   Your entire presence in your eyes
>   and the world turning slowly
> into a single branch of flame.

CONCLUSION

God's response to human affliction is rich and complex. If we think of the redeeming work of all three persons of the Trinity, each playing its own part in our healing and restoration, we recognize that God pours out a variety of graces. Each of us partakes of those graces in our own way according to our own unique nature and our own particular need. But, for all of us, all three persons of the Trinity are working to sanctify our distress, to heal us, and to lead us into the ways of wisdom and compassion.

The Father/Mother God is the Serene Center of our reality, unshaken by whatever has happened. This God manifests as Eternity, as the ocean or the Ganges River, placing our hardships in a vast perspective. This God manifests as the sky over a battlefield, untorn by the bullets, unscathed by the artillery, untainted by the blood.

When people turn from the anxiety and turmoil of life to a still place, a centered awareness of inner peace, is that escapism? Is it fantasy? Is it infantile delusion? Yes — unless it is reconnecting with the deepest level of reality — unless the Father/Mother God is the Serene Center of Reality. Because God is that "still point of the turning world," we can find peace in the midst of anxiety. We can look up from the battlefield's carnage and see that the sky is still blue.

The Son and the Spirit are both modes of God's presence with us in the midst of our lives, on the battlefield, at our side. But they are with us in different ways. The Son is with us in each and every successive present moment, as fellow sufferer. He shares and understands our experience. This sharing makes him a consoling companion, but he is more than that. He has been through the ordeal and has won the victory. He gives us not just sympathy but hope. By loving us enough to join us in our affliction, the Son grounds our identities in being beloved of God. We are not just perpetual victims. By joining us in affliction, the Son makes a bridge between our human passion, our mortal suffering, and the Serene Center. The Son connects us to the Father by "liv[ing] and dy[ing] as one of us . . . to reconcile us to . . . the God and Father of all."[23]

We face affliction with the Son on our right hand and the Spirit on our left. While the Son goes with us to our cross, the Spirit raises us up from our tombs. The Spirit breathes life back into us. We stand back up like the bones in Ezekiel's valley. The Holy Spirit restores our life and gives us power, real strength not only to endure, but also to overcome.

The Spirit draws us outside obsession with our wounded selves and opens our hearts to care for, value, enjoy, appreciate and serve others. We "gain our lives by losing them," find ourselves by forgetting ourselves, and are raised to a life larger than we had previously imagined. The immense and incomprehensible power of the Spirit moves within us subjectively, and it moves around us in the circumstances of our lives. In both movements, the Spirit renews our hope and courage. This more abundant life, now lived for others in the Spirit, is a new way of being in the world. It is nothing less than a way of being in God, for we are now living the Son's manner of life; we are now living as children of God.

The combined action of the Triune God is mysteriously greater than the sum of its parts. The Serene Center, the Fellow Sufferer, and the Empowering Spirit together work in us a change that begins with the miracle of facing another day and ends in the joyful promise of Resurrection into the New and Endless Day.

REFLECTION QUESTIONS

1. In responding to your own life challenges or in helping others, have you ever found yourself doing or saying helpful things you didn't know you had in you? How do you explain that?

2. Has suffering ever opened your heart to understand and care for others more deeply? If so, how?

3. Has serving others ever eased the pain in your own life? How did that happen?

4. When you pray, how does the Holy Spirit participate in your prayer? How do you recognize the movement of the Spirit during prayer? Have you ever been surprised by thoughts or feelings during prayer?

5. Have you experienced what this chapter calls "gracious serendipity," the right person, word, book or opportunity coming along at just the right moment to give you hope or somehow sustain you in a hard time?

NOTES

[1] John 3: 8.

[2] The word from the Latin versions of the Creed, *immensus*, is used to describe the Spirit as incomprehensible, meaning it "cannot be measured or contained in the categories of finite thought." John Macquarrie, *Paths In Spirituality* (Harrisburg: Morehouse Publishing, 1992), p. 42.

[3] Edwards said, "The affections are no other than the more vigorous and sensible exercises of the inclination and will of the soul . . . And though the affections have not their seat in the body, yet the constitution of the body, may very much contribute to the present emotion . . . And the degree of religion is rather to be judged by the fixedness and strength of the habit that is exercised in affection, whereby holy affection is habitual, than by

the degree of the present exercise. . ." Jonathan Edwards, "A Treatise Concerning Religious Affections," in *A Jonathan Edwards Reader*, ed. John E. Smith, Harry S. Stout, and Kenneth P. Minkema (New Haven: Yale University Press, 1995), pp. 141, 146.

4   Another too-small view of the Holy Spirit appears in Barth's evangelical theology, in which the Word (Scripture, Jesus and Preaching) is seen as the be-all and end-all of God's manifestation to us. Barth reduces the Spirit to the role of a receiver inside us. "The Spirit is the subjective side of the event of revelation." Karl Barth, *Church Dogmatics I.1* trans. G. W. Bromiley. (Edinburgh, 1975), p. 449. True enough, the Spirit is essential to a holy interpretation of the revelation we receive. Barth's view is just an incomplete picture. First, it limits the Spirit too much to what happens inside us and fails to account for the Spirit as a larger force in the world. Second, it defines the role of the Spirit as too passive. If we look back ever so briefly to scripture and the Christian tradition, we will see that the Spirit plays a far larger role in our healing and restoration than that of a passive receiver of revelation.

5   Paul calls the Holy Spirit "the Spirit of life" (echoing Genesis 1:2) and attributes the resurrection to that life-giving Spirit. "If the Spirit of him who raised Jesus from the dead dwells in you, he who raised Christ Jesus from the dead will give life to your mortal bodies through the Spirit which dwells in you." Romans 8: 11. Psalm 33:6, says, "By the word of the Lord the heavens were made, and all their hosts by the breath of his mouth . . ." Breath (*ruach*) is the word for Spirit.

6   Geoffrey Wainwright, "The Holy Spirit," in *The Cambridge Companion to Christian Doctrine*. ed. Colin E. Gunton (Cambridge: Cambridge University Press, 1997), pp. 274-275. In Luke-Acts, the Spirit motivates and empowers Jesus' ministry, then continues the same ministry of healing and reconciliation through the Apostles.

7   Romans 8:9.

8   "For all who are led by the Spirit of God are sons of God. For you did not receive the spirit of slavery to fall back into fear, but you have received the spirit of sonship. When we cry, 'Abba! Father!' it is the Spirit himself bearing witness with our spirit that we are children of God, and if children, then heirs, heirs of God and fellow heirs with Christ, *provided we suffer*

with him in order that we may also be glorified with him." Romans 8: 14-17.

9 In John Macquarrie's words, "The breath is the invisible . . . characteristic that distinguishes a living man from a dead one; . . . Spirit is the active, formative, life-giving power." John Macquarrie, *Paths In Spirituality*, p. 41.

10 On the one hand, making such an ultimate claim for the resurrection seems to require some clarification of what the resurrection actually is. On the other, that question calls for a book unto itself. Certainly there is the view of the resurrection as bodily in a literal sense. That could be a matter of sheer miracle and mystery, or it could be a matter of God crafting a new and perfected version of us from the form of our being preserved eternally in the Divine Mind. Or it could be a spiritual resurrection, the resurrection of the spiritual body of which Paul speaks in 1st Corinthians. Or it could be a life in the Whole in which individual identity falls away. Certainly much theology, especially Catholic theology, thinks in terms of union with God. This book will not take a position beyond this: Resurrection is of the person but to a new way of being, perhaps a transpersonal state somewhat as God is transpersonal; the resurrection is to a new order of life that transcends suffering.

11 John 14: 15.

12 William Temple, *Readings In John's Gospel*. (Wilton: Morehouse Barlow, 1939), p. 231.

13 John Macquarrie, *Principles of Christian Theology*, p. 333.

14 Gordon Kaufman, *God in the Face of Mystery* (Cambridge: Harvard University Press, 1993), pp. 264-280.

15 Luke 5: 13-19.

16 " 'Spirit' . . . may be described as the capacity for going out of oneself and beyond oneself, . . . for transcending oneself . . . The more man goes out from himself, the more the spiritual dimension of his life is deepened, the more he becomes truly man, the more he grows into the likeness of God who is Spirit. On the other hand, the more he turns inward and encloses himself in self-interest, the less human does he become." John Macquarrie, *Paths In Spirituality*, pp. 44-45.

17 David Kelsey, pp. 55-59.

18 Galatians 5: 19, 22.

19 "The Spirit is not only the bond of love, but also the one who breaks the bonds of self-love . . . . In this way the Holy Spirit indeed perfects the love of God, immanently and economically (as Family and Job-Description Trinity): immanently, by completing it as love . . . .; and economically, by being the differentiation, and perfection of divine love 'outward,' whereby, graciously, it opens out to address freely . . . the otherness of creation, and invest it with boundless difference, endless inflections of divine glory." Hart, *The Beauty of the Infinite*, p. 176.

20 Rowan Williams, p. 124.

21 Suffering turns us inward into a spasm of solitude. But the Spirit expands our awareness and concern into the diversity of others. The Spirit opens our hearts to experience the diversity of creation as redeeming beauty. An example would be the joy of observing the delightful multiplicity of form and color among the species of fish at an aquarium. In this sense, Jonathan Edwards called the diversifying Spirit, "the beautifier, the one in whom the happiness of God overflows, the one who bestows radiance, shape, clarity, and enticing splendor. . . ." Jonathan Edwards, *Miscellanies*, in *The Philosophy of Jonathan Edwards* ed. Harvey G. Townsend (Westport: Greenwood Press, 1972), p. 260; paraphrased by Hart, *The Beauty of the Infinite*, p. 178.

22 Romans 8: 14-15.

23 *The Book of Common Prayer* of the Episcopal Church, Eucharistic Prayer A, p. 362.

CHAPTER 12

MIRRORING GOD:
HOW WE RESPOND TO SUFFERING

Christ has no body on earth but yours
No hands, no feet on earth but yours
Yours are the eyes with which he looks
Compassion on this world.
— St. Theresa of Avila

In an old Pontius Puddle cartoon, one character says, "Sometimes I'd like to ask God why he doesn't do something about war, famine, disease, injustice and pollution."

"Why," the other replies, "don't you just ask him?"

The first character answers, "I'm afraid he might ask me the same question."

We have been asking in some depth what God does when we suffer. The more pressing question may be what we should be doing. How should we act in the face of our own adversities and those of others? Focusing exclusively on God's response makes for escapism and irresponsibility. If our faith is to make us strong, compassionate and resourceful, it is important that we consider how Christians are called to act in the face of adversity. In this chapter, we will look at the leading prescriptions for responding to suffering and then consider how a Trinitarian view of God can balance, enrich and diversify our ways of responding.

SUBMISSION

The attitude that all tribulations are to be borne with fatalistic acquiescence can be insidious. It can malign God, condone injustice, obstruct progress in alleviating suffering, and foster irresponsible passivity. Such servility is grounded in the false premise that God sends suffering either as punishment or for some other purpose.

On the other hand, there is suffering we cannot escape and cannot overcome. That is the time to pray the first petition of Reinhold Niebuhr's "Serenity Prayer," "God grant me the grace to accept those things I cannot change." When we accept suffering, we are accepting that for now this suffering is part of life, and we must take the bitter with the sweet, that life is, as the Buddha said, "10,000 joys and 10,000 sorrows" woven inseparably together.

There are two distinctions between Christian acceptance and fatalistic submission. Christians accept suffering only for now. Our long-run hope makes acceptance a matter of patience rather than despair.[1] Second, we accept only that we cannot change the situation, not that the situation cannot be changed. Although God is not dominating the world, God is involved in it; and we set no limits on what wonders God may be able to achieve. We do not expect miracles, but we hope for them.

STOICISM

We have done much and can do more to overcome various forms of suffering. That is all good. When we face evil that can be overcome, it is time to pray, "God grant me the courage to change what should be changed." The Millennium Development Goals for eradicating severe poverty throughout the world are a prime example.

But our success in overcoming so many of our ancient ills has given us the grandiose illusion that we can overcome all suffering with the right mix of spirituality and technology. We are tempted to believe life should be pain free, and when we find that it isn't, we think something is dreadfully amiss. Douglas John Hall calls this "the incapacity to suffer."[2] Stoicism is the practice of subjectively disengaging from painful situations in order to avoid suffering. Theologians call this assumption that suffering is avoidable and must always be avoided apathy.[3] By "apathy," we don't what is normally understood by the word. We don't mean not caring. We draw on the literal meaning of the word "non-suffering." Post-Christian society is unwilling to suffer, is committed to avoiding pain at all costs. Dorothee Soelle writes:

> One wonders what will become of a society in which certain forms of suffering are avoided gratuitously, In keeping with middle-class ideals... a society in which: a marriage that is perceived as unbearable

quickly and smoothly ends in divorce; after divorce no scars remain; relationships between generations are dissolved as quickly as possible, without a struggle, without a trace; periods of mourning are "sensibly" short; with haste the handicapped and sick are removed from the house and the dead from the mind . . . From suffering nothing is learned and nothing is to be learned.

Such blindness is possible in a society in which a banal optimism prevails, in which it is self-evident that suffering doesn't occur. . . In the equilibrium of the suffering-free state the life curve flattens out completely so that even joy and happiness can no longer be experienced intensely.[4]

We pay a high price for the denial of suffering. We deny life along with it. I once read a poem by a young woman writing about her pain over a failed attempt at love. She described meditating with the person she wanted but could not have, and she called her desire and her hurt "only thoughts." Sometimes we have to do such things to manage our pain, but ultimately such a practice reduces our whole life to "only thoughts." Even the label "only thoughts" is only a thought. Life is given us to be lived, not trivialized, reduced to something less than it is. Our pain is pain. Our joy is joy.

Real life is a combination of joys and sorrows. They are linked, dependent on each other like light and dark. If we anesthetize ourselves to the sorrows, we sacrifice the joys as well. Moreover, even when we are able to keep our heads and hearts above the waters of sorrow, others will not be so fortunate. If we are unwilling to suffer, then we must keep aloof from their experience. We must leave them to suffer alone.

Apathy cuts us off first from our own experience, then from the experience of our fellow mortals. Since some forms of suffering are inherent in being human, apathy amounts to denial of our humanity and repression of our actual experience. Hall observes that when we repress our suffering, we wind up inflicting the unacknowledged pain on those near to us and that we disable ourselves from imaginatively entering into the suffering of others.[5]

Much of what goes by the name "spirituality" today, in Christian and non-Christian circles alike, amounts to a Stoic attempt to render oneself impermeable to pain. Meditation is often reduced to relaxation exercises to reduce stress. Contemplation is imagining a pleasant place and pretending one is there instead of in the emotionally mixed reality of one's actual life. Prayer is an incantation to drive away our hardships; and faith is positive thinking. Expecting a miracle allows us to delay facing the reality at hand.

There is certainly a legitimate place in Christian practice for prayer and meditation that can open our hearts to solace and grace. However, in our current culture of apathy, there is grave danger of making a religion out of feel-good techniques. Such a religion is escapist and ultimately life-denying.

REBELLION

Albert Camus prescribed "metaphysical rebellion" as the most authentically human response to the futility of life.

Metaphysical rebellion is the movement by which man protests against his condition and against the whole of creation... The slave protests against... his state of slavery; the metaphysical rebel protests against ...his state as a man.[6]

We can easily generalize our experience of suffering, especially when it seems senseless, into a rebellion against the entire human condition. It is possible to respond to any tragedy with Romeo shouting, "then I defy you stars." We can shake our fists at the heavens, blame God, and stand as rebels against God.

The problem with rebellion as it is usually practiced is that it is an ego-assertion. Augustine saw such ego-assertion as the very thing that distorts our love and makes a mess of our lives . Put bluntly, "it's all about me." If God were the Cosmic Patriarch, rebellion would be heroic, Promethean. But we have already dismissed that image of God as infantile and false. Does that negate Camus' philosophy of revolt? No. Camus was not prescribing an infantile revolt against an infantile God image. He was too intelligent, too sophisticated, and too serious a philosopher for that. He was, however, quite clear that rebellion sets one over against reality itself. The price we pay for such a stance is that rebellion cuts one off from life and from others.

Camus tried to overcome the narcissism of rebellion by insisting that authentic rebellion must always be asserted in solidarity with humankind. The problem is the basis on which we build solidarity. Solidarity is a matter of identification. Rebels establish solidarity by identifying with each other because they are suffering the same injustice. They identify with their shared suffering. This identification with tragedy is precisely the pathological stuckness that makes for a suffocating spiritual prison.[7] Identification with old afflictions shuts down the dynamic flow of life, cuts us off from new experience. To form a false community based on such a shared identity only sets this pathology in concrete. Identification based on common affliction is an entirely different dynamic from compassion. Compassion for fellow sufferers motivates us to help each other to move on, to overcome. Identification, however, makes stuckness in sorrow a mark of group loyalty.

When taken to Camus' grand scale, we would identify with each other based on the general futility and meaninglessness of human life. Christians, however, insist that life is not ultimately futile or meaningless. Rather, the meaning is mysterious and is found in God. The journey into God is the journey toward meaning. To endure futility is to abandon the journey before it is well begun.

TRINITARIAN RESPONSE

The Christian response to suffering starts with our faith in God, specifically in the Triune God who is engaging our suffering as we have been describing. We respond to suffering with God and as God responds. God, as the foundation of Reality, is not escapist. God is intimately aware of reality, including its painful aspects.[8] Liberation theologian Jon Sobrino defines spirituality as "a fundamental willingness to face what is real" — including the realities of pain and injustice.[9] There is no room for escapism or naive optimism in the Christian response.

SERENITY

My life flows on in endless song
Above earth's lamentation
I hear the sweet and far off hymn
That hails a new creation.
Through all the tumult and the strife
I hear the music ringing
It finds an echo in my soul
How can I keep from singing? . . .
No storm can shake my inmost calm
While to that rock I'm clinging

Since Christ is Lord of heaven and earth
How can I keep from singing?
— Robert Lowry, "How Can I Keep from Singing?"

While we face head on the harsh realities of life and death, we set them in the transcendent context of eternity, the essence of which is God's infinite peace. We believe with Paul that the sufferings of this present time are not worth comparing to the glories that are to be revealed. That does not mean we dismiss the sufferings of today or fail to take them seriously. But we do place them in a larger context of hope.

We are able to grieve the more fully because we know that grief is not the end. It will not swallow us. Life will swallow up death. We fully experience our own pain, but we don't succumb to it, because we hope for redemption. We can also care for others without taking on their despair. In fact, our serenity, born of faith and hope, can lift others up from despair. We can be non-anxious because of our trust that God will redeem.

Our hope has its eyes set on the Serene Center. Christians, at our best, remember eternity. We remember that God's love is the only thing that lasts. With that faith, we cling to our hope even in the midst of tears. Christian faith calls us to live into hope, not despair. We are not naive. We operate under no illusions. But we hold fast to the knowledge that God is always present working in all situations, luring them toward peace, justice, and healing. We work and pray for miracle and wonder to happen right now. When it happens, we praise God. When it doesn't, we set our hope in eternity.

COMPASSION

Our own suffering is not diminished but it is transformed by the compassion of the Son. There is the danger of becoming absorbed in our individual grief, loneliness or despair. But, Christ shares our experience to give us another way. We can let our suffering become a point of connection. That is the spirituality of the Cross. The Way of the Cross does not render us impermeable to pain. Rather, it makes pain a part of our process of salvation.

The way of the Cross doesn't invite suffering. We don't have to do that. It comes uninvited. But we don't run from it. We use our hardships as the raw material of compassion. The world suffers. People nearby are sick, imprisoned, lonely, poor and afraid. People around the world face famine, war, epidemics, and political oppression. The Way of the Cross refuses to imagine all that away. It connects our individual pain with the suffering of the world. It makes of suffering a Communion, the body of Christ, broken and shared to make us all one.

Jesus' way isn't to cling masochistically to our pain as if it made us special. It doesn't. We all have our fair share of sorrow. Jesus' way is to make our pain a point of connection to each other so we actually don't think so much about ourselves. We don't fret over whether we are as happy as we deserve to be. When we walk through our sorrow boldly and compassionately, like Jesus and with Jesus, instead trying to find a by-pass around it, that's when the miracle happens. We lose our life to in order to find it.

Our response to the suffering of others is to see that it is just as important as our own. We share the experience, and in our compassion we do whatever is in our power to alleviate other people's pain. We devote whatever spiritual gifts we have received to their service. To us, every suffering person is Jesus on the Cross. When we live as Christ lived, even in the midst of our own hardships and those of others, there is a stream of grace flowing, the grace of compassion which is at once human and divine. Nicholas Wolterstorff writes:

Mourn humanity's mourning, weep over humanity's weeping, be wounded by humanity's wounds, be in agony over humanity's agony. But do so in the good cheer that a day of peace is coming.[10]

We become like the God we worship. We join our God in mission to the world. So when we response to the world's pain, our response is the same as God's. Douglas John Hall says of God's response:

... (T)he magnitude of the suffering that we actually see about us in the world should not be! .... Dostoevsky's Ivan Karamazov himself is not more sensitive to the wrongness of all this than is the God of Sinai and Golgotha. Like Jesus regarding Jerusalem from a little distance, our Scriptures bear witness to a god who weeps over the tragedies of earth — even over our little losses. (Matt. 10: 30, par.) This God will not rest until the wrong of suffering has been righted — until death itself is defeated. (Rev. 21:4).[11]

Paul said, "I want to share in the sufferings of Christ . . . ." He was

MIRRORING GOD: HOW WE RESPOND TO SUFFERING

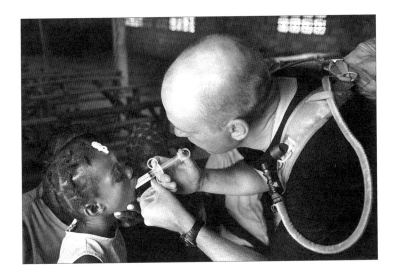

talking about Communion, not as a ritual but as a way of life. We are the Body of Christ that is broken at the altar. Our lives are his blood poured out. In suffering, we are made one with each other and one with God. But Christian compassion is different from Camus' solidarity in rebellion because we have more in common than our shared suffering. We understand each other to be beloved children of God. We see each other and ourselves as infinitely valuable and precious. We share not just common affliction, but common hope. Wolterstorff says,

> We are one in suffering.... God is love. That is why he suffers. To love our suffering world is to suffer.... So suffering is down at the center of things, deep down where the meaning is. For Love is the meaning. And Love suffers. The tears of God are the meaning of history... We're in it together, God and we, together in the history of our world.[12]

REDEEMING, EMPOWERING ACTION

Thanks to the action of the Holy Spirit, we do not have to rely on our inner resources alone to be resilient when things go wrong. The Spirit raises us up, restores our life, and gives us strength. In facing our own hardships, God does more than suffer with us. God gives us the power to survive and flourish and to live in the Spirit. The Spirit draws us outside ourselves into concern for others.

Photo: A medical augmentee gives a child medication during disaster relief efforts in Haiti. / Joshua Adam Nuzzo, U.S. Navy Specialist Apprentice.

When the Spirit raises us from the dust of despair, we become agents of the Spirit, channels of blessing, "instruments of God's peace," carrying grace to others. We respond to their need, not just by feeling what they feel, not just by hurting with them, but also by giving them hope. Sometimes hope is just an encouraging word, but more often it takes the form of concrete action, doing something of practical service. John said, "Let us love not in word or speech but in deed and in truth."[13]

There is nothing sentimental about the spiritual life, the life of love. It is hard because, even right here and now in this broken world, we have been given the grace to love. But our love has not yet been given the power to achieve its purpose. Sometimes, by luck or grace, love actually prevails, but it is far from guaranteed to "conquer all." In the face of divisions of race and religion, love often fails. We pour our love out like water over a rock. The world does not love itself enough to accept our love. And our failed attempts at love tempt us despair of the effort. Blaming the world for its failure to love or accept love is unfair and pointless. The truth is the world is broken and love does not fare well in it. Yet love persists. This experience of love's seeming futility is why we live by hope. Hugh Martin said of love and hope in Robert Browning's poetry:

The pity and love which make men revolt against suffering and evil were implanted in them by their Creator, who must be at least as good as His creatures. The evil in the world is there to be overcome, and it can be overcome. Love is active in the world: and who put it there? One day love will have the irresistible power it deserves to have.[14]

We live in hope of that day.

THE SANDY HOOK ELEMENTARY SCHOOL MASSACRE

Through the years of writing this book, tragedies have compounded, each one forcing me back to the existential drawing board — seeing my text on the computer screen exposed as pitifully inadequate in the face of flesh and blood sorrow. There have been natural evils — 230,000 killed in the Haiti earthquake of 2010; 70,000 killed in the Sichuan quake of 2008; the Pakistan flood of 2012; the Japan earthquake, tsunami and Fukushima nuclear disaster of 2012. There have been human evils — atrocities in the Congo and Sudan; mass shootings at Virginia Tech, Ft. Hood, the Aurora Theater, the Sikh Temple, Tucson, and a one-room Amish school to name just a few.

As this book goes to press, we have also witnessed the mass murder of elementary school children and their teachers at Sandy Hook Elementary School in Connecticut. Again the question, "Where was God?" Again many interpretations are drawn. Absurd things are said, like "this is God's punishment for the absence of prayer in schools."

This book has not prescribed a neat formula to which such a thing can be reduced. The tragedy at Sandy Hook Elementary demonstrates that evil will not be reduced to any neat formula. But I will do my best to offer a glimpse into how the Trinitarian God responds and calls us to respond to horrific evils.

The closer we are to this loss, the more we need to access some firm foundation of hope, like the music in Lowry's hymn:

My life flows on in endless song
Above earth's lamentation
I hear the sweet and far off hymn
That hails a new creation.
Through all the tumult and the strife
I hear the music ringing . . .

The bereaved need a God of Eternity to hold their grief. We all do. And they need people who embody that faith for them when it is hard to find hope in their own broken hearts.

If we love our children as much as is humanly possible, God loves them infinitely. If we suffer at their deaths, God suffers infinitely. The Cross happened again in Newtown, Connecticut. We meet God at that Cross, the God who will someday redeem and resurrect. The victims need a God who joins them, who goes all the way into the hell of death and grief with them. And they need people who embody God's compassion, who, in Wolterstorff's words, "Mourn humanity's mourning, weep over humanity's weeping, [are] wounded by humanity's wounds . . . ." In the moment of loss, it is possible to find God precisely because in that moment we can find each other.

The friends and parents of the slain children and teachers will need more than hope and compassion to find their way into a future. They will need that mysterious infusion of strength and courage the Spirit offers. They will need the meaning-making process of spiritual growth and transformation — an inner process manifesting outwardly in life for others. That meaning-making will take different forms for each person.

The public discourse in the wake of the Sandy Hook Elementary massacre is a desperate scramble to make meaning out of senseless loss. People are proposing gun control, improved school security, expanded access to mental health, and other ways to improve society, mostly good enough ideas. But to me they all seem too small, too utilitarian. Tragedy of this magnitude calls for more than a technical fix to reduce the likelihood of it happening again. The best way to invest with meaning the wave of mass murders we have experienced in recent years would be to repent from social violence. Reasonable regulation of firearms would be the most obvious pragmatic way to back off from our compulsive habit of violence. But gun reform is a far, far cry from enough on the one hand, and extraordinarily hard to achieve on the other.

Our societal violence goes much deeper than legislation can reach. More than any other developed nation, we have embraced the meta-narrative the late Walter Wink called "the myth of redemptive violence." The myth he describes is an ancient story line beginning with the Enuma Elish, the Sumerian creation myth. Marduk, one of several Sumerian gods, becomes king of the gods because of his combat skills. He slays the sea monster Tiamat and creates the heavens from her body. The import of the Enuma Elish, as Wink reads it, is that meaning, value, and heroism lie in killing the enemy. Wink offered the gospel of Jesus Christ as the counter-narrative of "redemptive love."

But for every movie, book, and TV program valorizing a Christ figure, there are 100 valorizing a Marduk figure. The catechism of American culture is a course in the myth of redemptive violence. So we live with fantasies of someday blowing away a villain. The myth of redemptive violence invests our human worth in our capacity to kill. So we, as a nation, invested our wealth in a nuclear arsenal that would destroy every living person on earth many times over. We incarcerate more people than any other developed nation. Unlike most modern democracies, we persist with the death penalty. From the video games we sell our children, to our sports, to our law enforcement, to our foreign policy, we embrace violence. In our pride and in our fear, we have made what Isaiah called "a covenant with death"— meaning we ground our safety and our self-esteem on our capacity to kill. Is it then any wonder that the psychologically vulnerable in a society that venerates violence, turn assault weapons on our people, killing federal judges, young adults at movie theaters, and first graders at their desks?

When I think of a transformation that would give some modicum of meaning to the blood shed by our children, nothing less than a societal conversion from a model of valor like Marduk to a model of valor like Jesus will do. The Sumerian creation myth says the universe is born in bloodshed; hence, the savior Marduk comes with guns blazing. The Jewish creation myth says the universe is procreated by a parental God who says "It is good;" hence, the Savior Jesus comes in love, even sacrificial love.

So to draw the circle to a close, that is what this book has been about — the discovery of a better God, the kind of God manifest in a Jesus — not Marduk — a God of serenity, compassion, and relational power to live for others.

CONCLUSION

We can practice a wise, compassionate and courageous response to suffering if we keep our Trinitarian theology straight. Those who worship only the Serene Father (though these days they are more apt to call him "the Tao," "Dharma," "the One," "non-duality," "emptiness," or some such impersonal abstraction) will be inclined to either submit to suffering or avoid it. Those who worship only the Compassionate Son will be inclined to indulge in suffering, both directly and vicariously, thinking such indulgence ennobles them and makes them Christ-like. Those who worship only the Spirit will believe all suffering can be eradicated if we can just work up enough faith and enthusiasm.

But a balanced faith in the Triune God balances our response to suffering. We have the wisdom to accept that some suffering is a given part of life for now, but that in eternity "all will be well." Our relationship with the Serene Father enables us to be the "non-anxious presence" who helps others by hearing them with serenity and equanimity. Our relationship with the Son enables us to embrace our own suffering directly and to respond compassionately to the suffering of others. And in the power of the Spirit, we protest against unnecessary suffering and strive to alleviate it wherever we can. Balancing all three approaches takes wisdom, which we spend a lifetime cultivating. It is not easy, but Augustine taught that the Triune God is already reflected in the Trinitarian structure of our souls. So when we respond to suffering in a Trinitarian way, with Serene Wisdom, Vulnerable Compassion, and Life-giving Encouragement, our response is both effective and authentic.

REFLECTION QUESTIONS

1. What are the advantages and disadvantages of submission, apathy, rebellion and love as responses to suffering?

2. St. Theresa of Avila said, "Pray as if it all depended on God. Work as if it all depended on you." Is that good advice in dealing with suffering?

3. How does faith in the Serene Center, the companionship of the Compassionate Son, and the Empowerment of the Spirit affect the way we serve others in times of trouble?

NOTES

1   St. Paul said in Romans 8 that "the sufferings of this present time are not worth comparing to the glory which will be revealed." It is in that spirit of waiting that we accept suffering.

2   Douglas John Hall at p. 41.

3   Dorothee Soelle and Douglas John Hall both use the term "apathy" with this meaning.

4   Dorothee Soelle, at pp. 38-39.

5   Douglas John Hall, pp. 41-47.

6   Albert Camus, *The Rebel*, trans. Anthony Bower (New York: Alfred A. Knopf, 1956), p. 23.

7   David Kelsey, pp. 55-59.

8   Rowan Williams says God lives "with and within the potentially hurtful and destructive bounds of the world." He also says, "the Spirit connects us to reality in a way that bridge[s] . . . the gulf between suffering and hope . . . confronting suffering without illusion but also without despair." Rowan Williams, p. 124.

9   Mark A. MacIntosh, *Mystical Theology* (Oxford: Blackwell Publishers, 1998), pp. 28-29.

10   Nicholas Wolterstorff, p. 86.

11   Douglas John Hall, at pp. 74-75.

12   Nicholas Wolterstorff, pp. 89-91.

13   1 John 3: 17.

14   Hugh Marin, *The Faith of Robert Browning* (London: SCM Press Ltd., 1963), p. 94.

About the Author

Dan Edwards grew up in rural Texas, earned his B. A. and J. D. at the University of Texas, then moved to Colorado where he practiced Migrant Law for three years. He went on to practice law for another nine years in Idaho before attending the General Theological Seminary where he earned his M. Div. and an S.T.M. in Spiritual Direction. As a young adult he practiced Buddhism and was social justice activist, but never was able to reconcile his spirituality with his politics. His return to Christianity coincided with his despair over the possibilities of social action. But 9/11 forced him to rethink the role of religion in the social and political order. A Merrill Fellowship at Harvard Divinity School and a Guthrie Scholarship at Columbia Theological Seminary gave him an opportunity to start rethinking the socio-political implications of Christian theology and spiritual practice. The writing of this book has been a decade-long process of thinking aloud as he has been revising his beliefs and prayer life to a channel for God's grace, as he works with community organizing efforts to make the world more just and merciful. The process is on-going.

He has published a few scholarly articles, but this is his first book. His poetry has been published by Sacred Journey, Ars Poetica, and the Austin Poetry Society Newsletter. Dan Edwards currently serves as the 10th Bishop of Nevada, after having been a parish priest in Macon, Georgia for 18 years.

Photo: Dan Edwards / Used with permission.